OMNIBUS PRESS PRESENTS THE STORY OF

KORN

Y0-EIL-850

Copyright © 2000 Omnibus Press
(A Division of Book Sales Limited)

Written by Doug Small
Cover/Book Design by
Sun-Jaia Romigin

US ISBN: 0.8256.1804.5
UK ISBN: 0.7119.8434.4

Exclusive distributors:
Book Sales Limited
8/9 Frith Street, London
W1V 5TZ, UK.

Music Sales Corporation
257 Park Avenue South
New York City, NY 10010, USA

Music Sales Pty LTD.
120 Rothschild Avenue
Rosebery, NSW 2018
Australia

To the Music Trade only:
Music Sales Limited.
8/9 Frith Street, London
London W1V 5TZ, UK.

All rights reserved. No part of this book may be reproduced in any form or by any electronic or mechanical means, including information storage or retrieval systems, without permission in writing from the the publisher, except by a reviewer who may quote brief passages.

Photo Credits:
Rodolphe Baras/LFI: 31
Bob Berg/Retna Ltd: 2/3,53,74
Kristin Callahan/LFI: 15,19,20,25,44,45,55,57
MB Charles/Retna Limited USA: 66
Kevin Estrada/Retna Limited USA: 67,75
Frank Forcino/LFI: 5,13,36
Eugene Gologursky/Retna Ltd: 32
Olly Hewitt/All Action/Retna: 61
Jen Lowery: 6,7,9,11,14,18,21,26,27,28,29,34,
37,39,41,43,46,47,50,51,52,54,58,80
Jen Lowery/LFI: 33,49
Sam Mack/Retna Limited USA: 60,69,70/71,79
Joseph Marzullo/Retna Limited USA: Title Page
John McMurtrie/Retna: 12,17
Brad Miller/Retna Limited USA: 65
Suzan Moore/All Action/Retna: 59
Joy E. Scheller/LFI: 23,62
George De Sota/LFI: 35,63
K. Swift/Retna: 38
Frank White: 73, 77

Front Cover Photograph: Bob Berg
Back Cover Photograph: Mick Hutson

Printed in the United States of America by
Vicks Lithograph and Printing Corp.

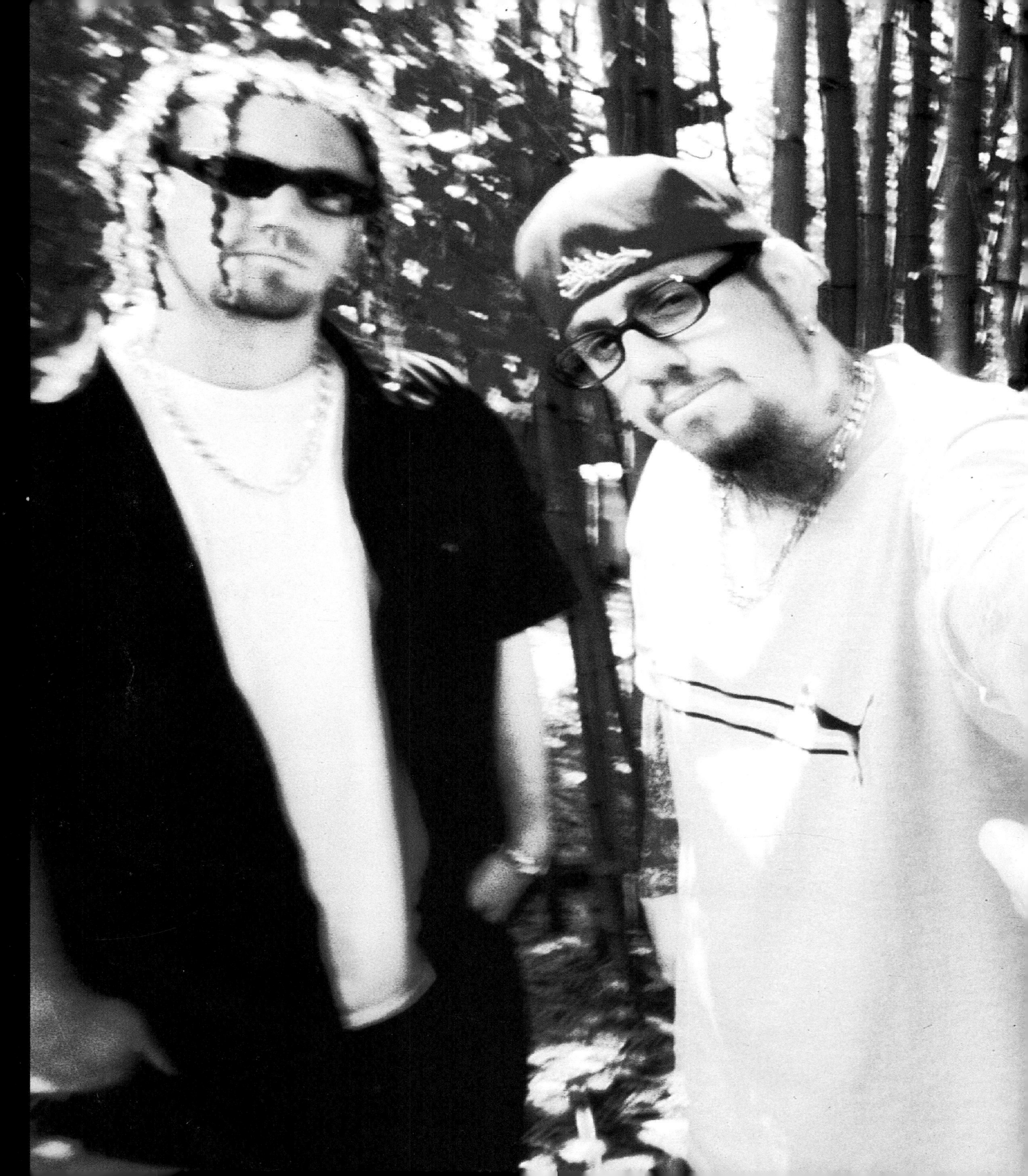

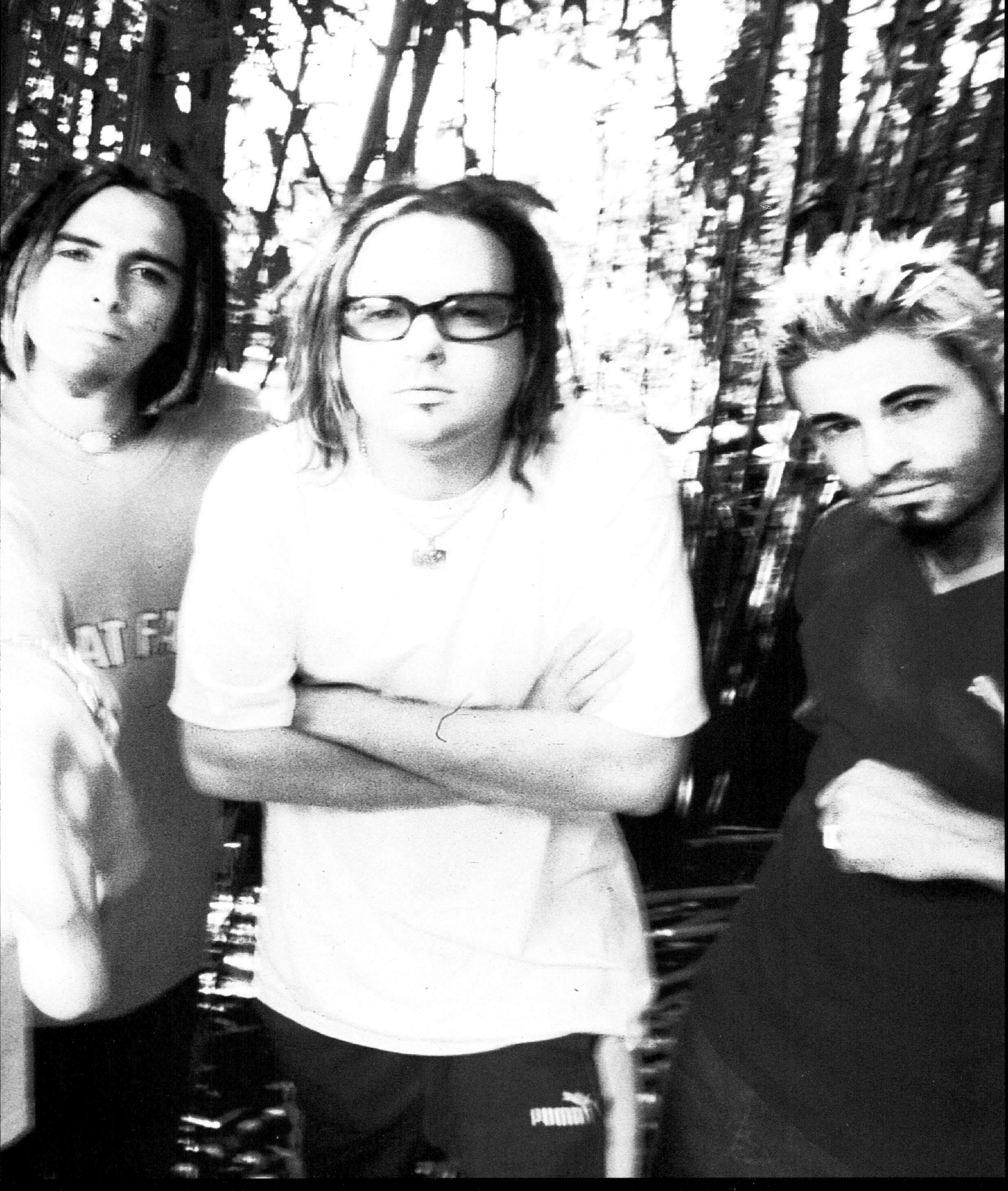
PUMA

WHAT THE HELL IS KORN?

An ingenious cross-pollination of metal, rock, hip-hop, deep grooves, dissonance, and hardcore? A demented chaotic assault on the senses? A bad influence that is leading today's youth astray, or a cathartic outlet for a generation's anger? The leader of the sonic revolution and the answer to the prayers of a tired, creatively bankrupt music scene? Even the five members of Korn are hard-pressed to define themselves, but as testified by their ever-growing and fiercely loyal fan base, whatever it is, it works. Like black magic.

The multidimensional sound of Korn is juxtaposition at its best. Each musician manages to at once contribute to the band's distinct sound and to stand out as a unique element; it is a rare accomplishment that Korn has somehow found a current that allows five singular, individual voices to present a unified sound that is all their own. Korn's signature dissonant heavy grooves are the work of guitarists James "Munky" Shaffer and Brian "Head" Welch. Two outrageously inventive seven-string players who, rather than solo, play off one another to unprecedented effect are a lethal combination. Add to this bassist Reggie "Fieldy" Arvizu's fingerstyle groove, heavy slapping techniques, and unique clicking—much more than a conventional anchor for the two-guitar strong lead section, his playing creates a basis as freaky and fresh as the resulting sound of Korn. Drummer David Silveria is responsible for the hard-edged syncopation of Korn; his precision power drumming drives the insanity right on home. Top this all off with a lead singer whose gut-wrenching, tortured, over-the-edge and into-the-abyss vocals and shockingly candid lyrics are without compare. Jonathan Davis, the pissed-off prodigal son of metal and dysfunctional godchild of new wave, is the eye of the storm around which the music of Korn rages.

Korn is a basket-caseful of contradictions. The band almost single-handedly responsible for introducing the newest, heaviest brand of music to hit the MTV generation over the head has been known to play Lionel Ritchie's "Hello" at sound check, and their tour-bus CD collection features the likes of Blondie, Missing Persons, and *The Village People's Greatest Hits.* A band with its own internet television show, whose latest album debuted at Number One, Korn has had virtually no radio or video support. Their grassroots method of constant touring and word-of-mouth may well have been a catalyst to the high standards Korn sets for itself on stage. Or maybe they're just a kick-ass band who never has a bad night. Either way, Korn have gained a well-deserved reputation for putting on a consistently intense, tight, and hard show. Every time. They rock. Then they go home to their wives and families. Korn is all that. And much, much more ... in their own words, **"ARE YOU READY?"**

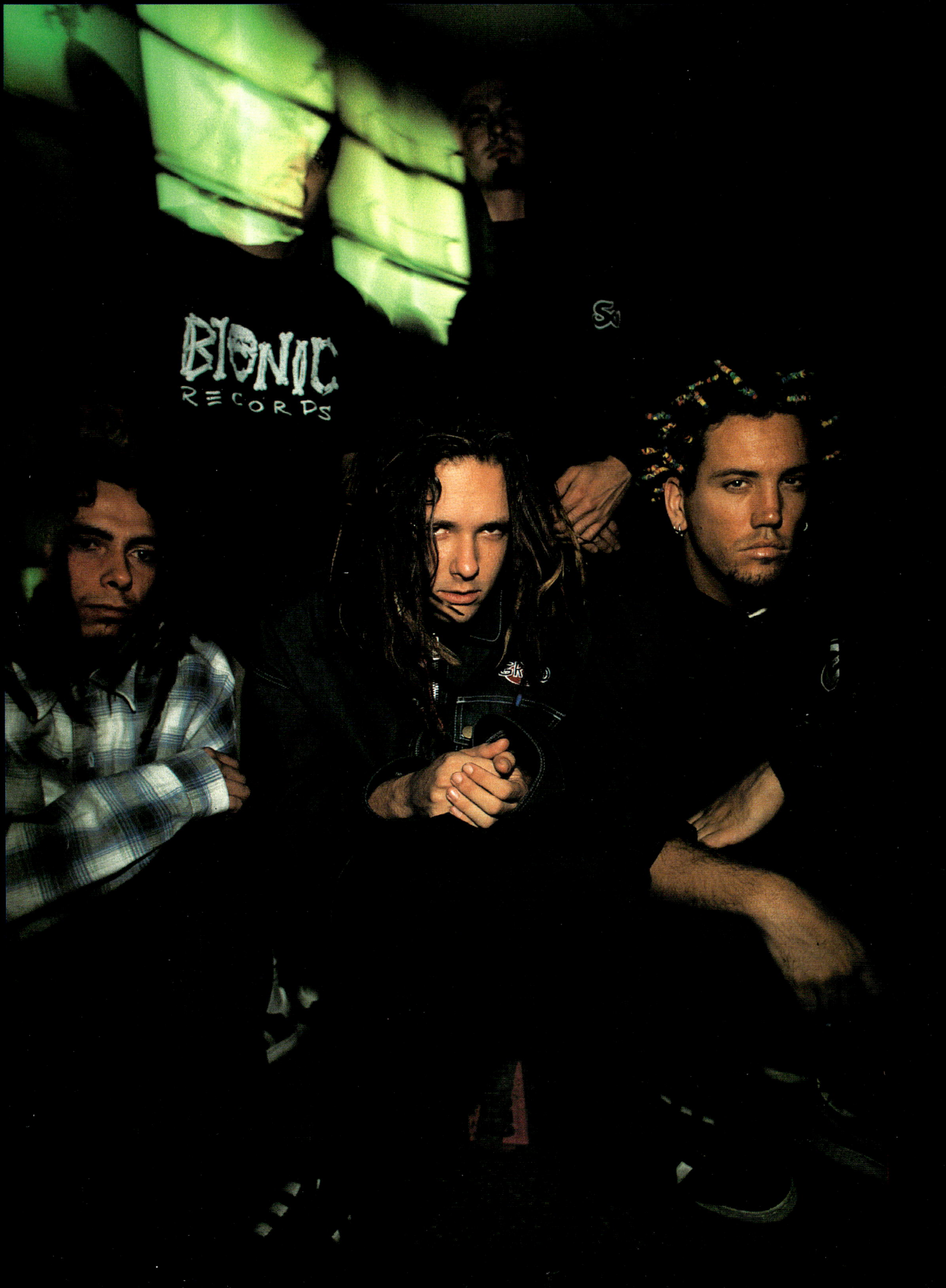
BIONIC
RECORDS

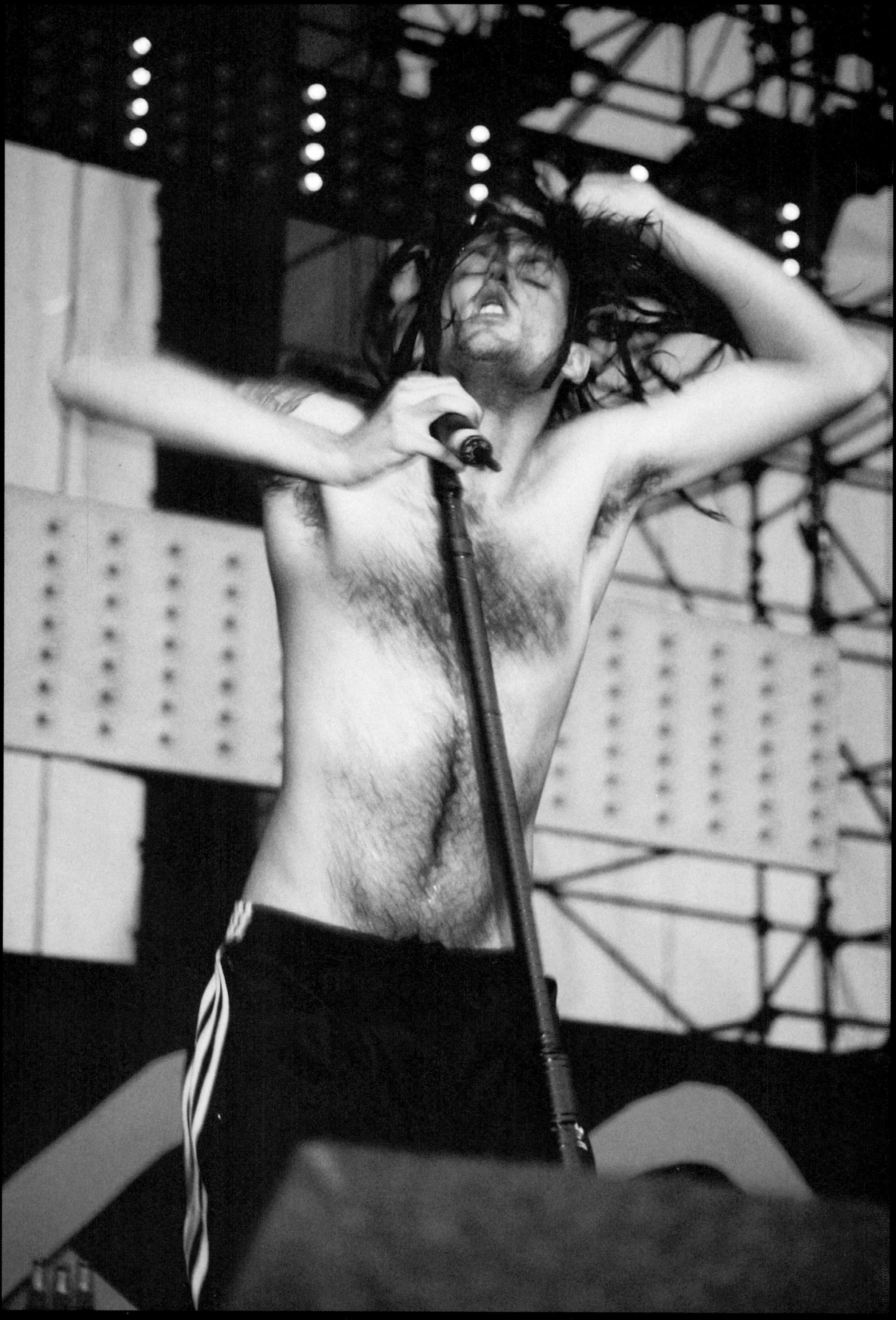

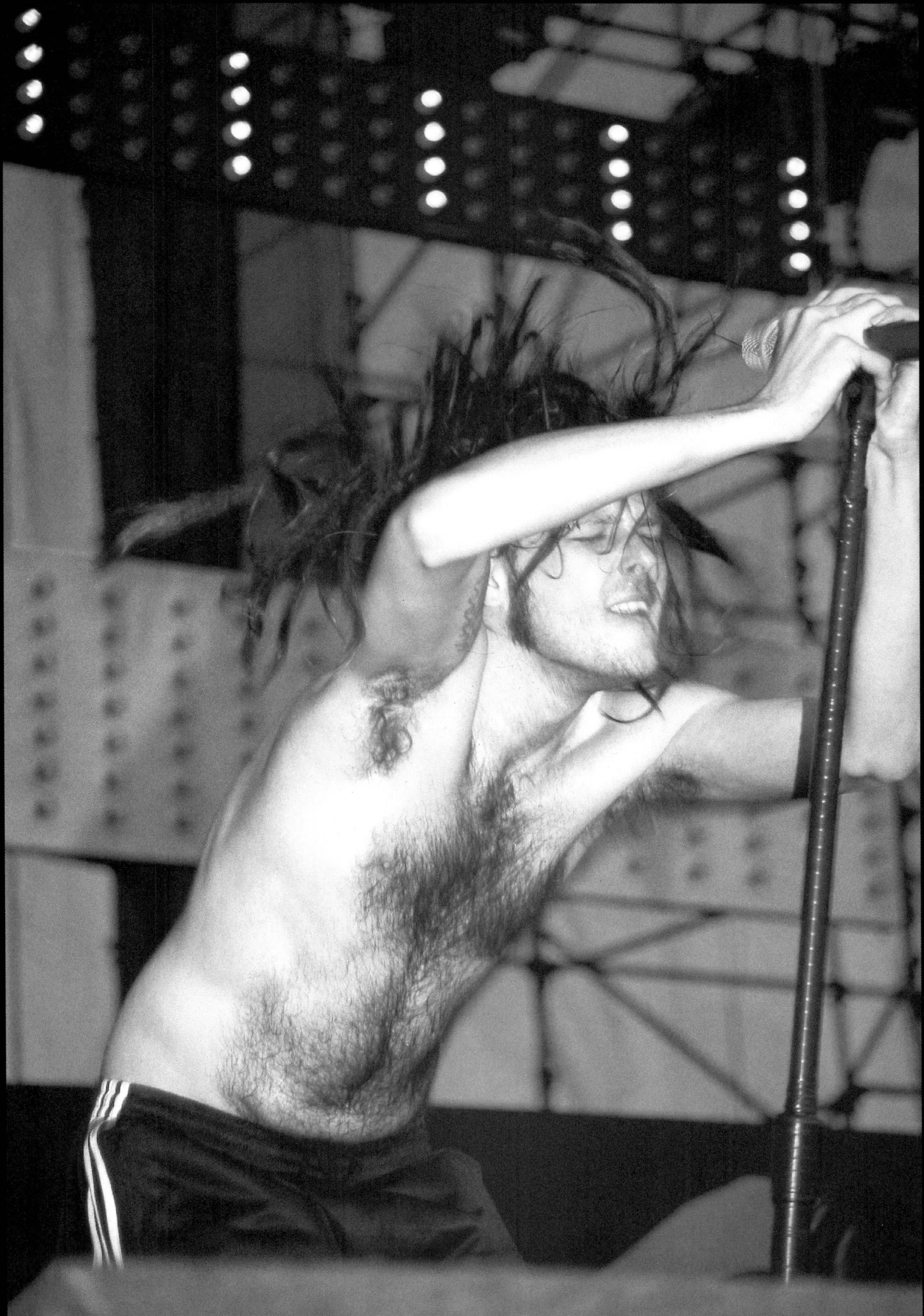

CHILDREN OF THE KORN

Southern California is the birthplace of many a successful band, and a myriad of unsuccessful ones. At the southern end of the San Joaquin Valley is a city called Bakersfield; it's not a place for which Korn and company profess much of the there's-no-place-like-home brand of love. Jonathan Davis put it succinctly enough when he told *Circus* magazine in August of 1996, "I hate that place with a passion. It's just evil there. It's horrible. There's nothing to do there for kids. The only thing you can do is join a gang or get fucked up on drugs, or get into music." Luckily for us, the future members of Korn chose the latter form of entertainment.

Agricultural, semi-rural Bakersfield, true to its name, has as one of its main features—you guessed it—a lot of fields. Teenagers make do with what they've got in more ways than one, and one of the favorite pastimes of the Bako youth was dirt field parties. Hundreds of kids would gather, light bonfires, and drink or do their drug of choice while gazing at the scenery (made up mainly of their own parked cars). Hanging out in a field getting wasted isn't as fun as it doesn't sound, and the inevitable burst of boredom-fueled violence was more often than not the highlight. After all, what's a good party without a fight? The seed of Korn, however, was planted in a burgeoning friendship between schoolmates Reggie "Fieldy" Arvizu and Brian "Head" Welch. With the help of their parents, who shuttled their respective sons back and forth between each other's houses so that they could fool around playing guitar, the two began a musical partnership and a deep-rooted friendship that would endure for years to come. Soon the guitar duo decided to form a band, and Brian recruited one James Shaffer.

James, who became known as Munky, had taken up the guitar on a real fluke; a three-wheeler accident cut off the tip of one of his fingers, and his doctor suggested he take up an instrument to rehabilitate the chopped digit. As Munky recalled his invitation to join up, he claimed in Korn's *Who Then Now?* "home video" that it "wasn't even if I could play or not, it was 'cause I had long hair!" Long hair or no, Munky fit the bill, and the threesome were jamming whenever they could, while putting the word out on the Bakersfield streets that they were in need of a drummer.

This is where David Silveria stepped in. Not, however, the built, good-looking, nipple-pierced, tattooed David of today—this David was, well, a bit on the young side. As Fieldy laughingly recounted in *Who Then Now?*, "I get this message on my machine—David's like, fuckin' thirteen. It's like (tiny voice) 'hey guys, looking for a drummer?' This little kid on my answering machine!" Despite their un-Hanson-like hesitation, the threesome quickly became a foursome once they discovered that the "little kid" could play the shit out of his drums. He had been pounding away since the ripe old age of nine. "I remember picking up the drums on my own and not being able to get my mind off them," he told *Modern Drummer* in April 1997.

The Korns-to-be got the hell out of Bakersfield, and moved to Huntington Beach. Munky, Fieldy, and David formed an official group they christened L.A.P.D. in honor, presumably, of the city's illustrious police department. Head, despite being on the scene, was not an L.A.P.D. band member, as the conventional one-guitar, bass, drums, and voice line-up was the word. Head and Munky continued their tradition of friendly competition, challenging each other's skills and motivating each player to go the extra mile each time they heard the other play.

L.A.P.D., with lead singer Richard Morales, released an album entitled *Who's Laughing Now* in 1991 on Triple X Records, as well as an earlier 1989 EP called *Love and Peace, Dude*. Triple X, an "indie" label jump-started in 1986 by record importers Peter Heur and Dean Naleway, was also home to Jane's Addiction and Cradle of Thorns. Right on the money, Triple X today claims to be based on "the philosophy that alternative music with a vision launches the musical trends of tomorrow." The label has recently re-released "the entire L.A.P.D. collection of songs compiled on one CD with all new graphics" in the wake of Korn's success. Of L.A.P.D.'s music, David would years later

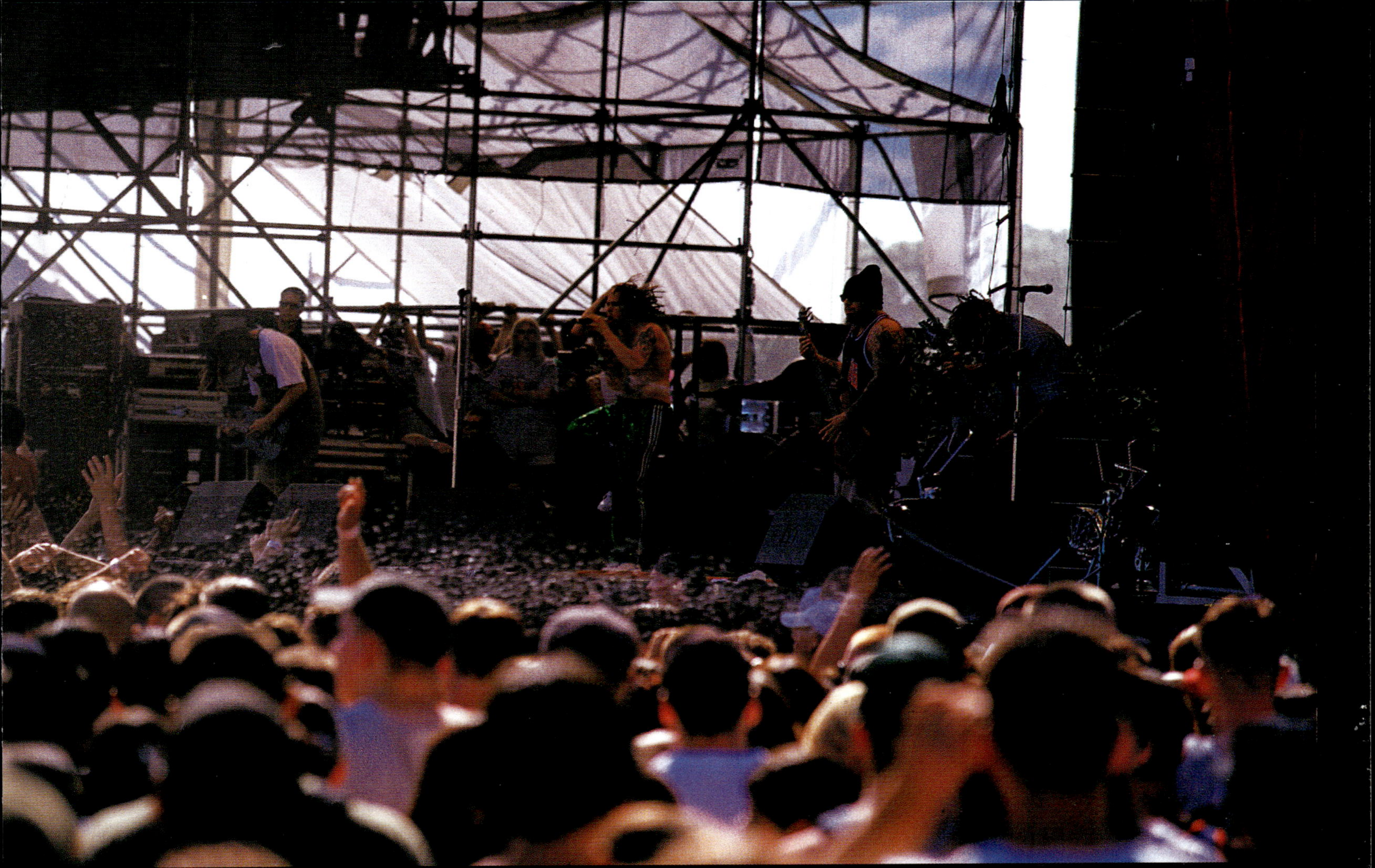

tell *Modern Drummer*, "we were still trying to find our own band sound and develop our own individual sounds on our instruments. If you listen to those records now, you wouldn't even think we were the same guys playing on them. It was kind of a heavy, up-tempo punk, not at all what we're doing now."

L.A.P.D. was busy playing the Los Angeles club circuit, either paying to play or playing for free. Head—presumably with the hard-won realization that while being in a struggling new band isn't exactly the gravy train, mooching around said struggling new band definitely won't pay the rent—was moments away from heading back to Bakersfield where he had a gig lined up pumping gas when L.A.P.D. split up, and the three remaining members asked him to formally join up with them to form a new group. They called it Creep. While the future Korn members were wetting their feet in the music industry and paying their dues, a certain Bakersfield native named Jonathan Davis was gaining a very different type of knowledge that would also, unbeknownst to him, become a vital part of Korn.

As any self-respecting Korn fan well knows, Jonathan Davis's childhood was ever so slightly difficult. Born on January 18, 1971, to a musician father and a mother who was an actress and dancer in local theater, the future Korn front man's troubles started early. When he was three his parents divorced and his father's subsequent remarriage to an evil stepmother Jonathan wasn't exactly thrilled to call "mom" (see his musical tribute to her in the form of Korn song "Kill You") didn't help matters. His dad was a keyboard player who was always on the road while his son was busy trying to grow up, and, prophetically enough, was bandmates with another local musician—Reggie "Fieldy" Arvizu's father. In fact, Fieldy claims to have been born on tour, forcing the band to make an unscheduled stop. Mr. Davis, Sr., was a member of then country music star Buck Owen's band, and although country music may not have been Jonathan's cup of Jägermeister at the time, he has since put forth that the Nashville exile was not uncool to have set up in Bakersfield, and that certain country tunes are true punk. Jonathan's father went on to own a music store and Owen's Bakersfield recording studio.

The young Davis, despite the fact that it was music that kept his father away from home so much of the time, was drawn to it, and studied classical music throughout his early years. He also got into the 80s new wave in a serious way; his favorite band was Duran Duran. While most Bakersfield dudes into music were trying to impress chicks with guitars and amps, he, in typically unconventional mode, took up the bagpipes due in part to a bit of Scottish lineage, and found the rather difficult instrument to be to his liking. Going against the grain suited our hero, and he did it in style, rushing into the school bathroom as soon as his 'rents dropped him off in the morning in order to put on his makeup. The Max Factor face, together with a penchant for wearing women's clothes, actually landed him in the guidance counselor's office on one occasion, but after assuring the powers that be that he was neither gay nor trying to cause trouble, he was sent back out into the hallways. Jonathan would later write a song about the constant taunting and abuse he endured throughout his school days for the high school code's mortal sins of nonconformity and individuality. "Faget," a relentless rave, asks, "All my life, who am I? A faget!"

When he wasn't sighting ghosts, Jonathan, at the tender age of fifteen, got his kicks from driving over the Grapevine freeway overpass into L.A. to check out bands. His very first such gig was a group called Cradle of Thorns. Not in a million years would Jonathan then have guessed that he was listening to a band that would years later release an album on the future lead singer's very own record label.

With the resolution not to follow in his father's footsteps firmly in mind, Jonathan Davis made yet another unconventional life choice and decided to launch a career as far removed from music as possible. His field of choice? Death. He enrolled in San Francisco's School of Mortuary Science, where he successfully earned a degree, and picked up a little gig at the California Kern County Coroner's Department. He was an Assistant Coroner. In his free time he performed stints on a freelance basis as an undertaker at a local funeral home. Jonathan's experiences during those years were beyond comprehension. In a horribly candid, pained moment, Jonathan revealed to *Alternative Press*'s John Pecorelli

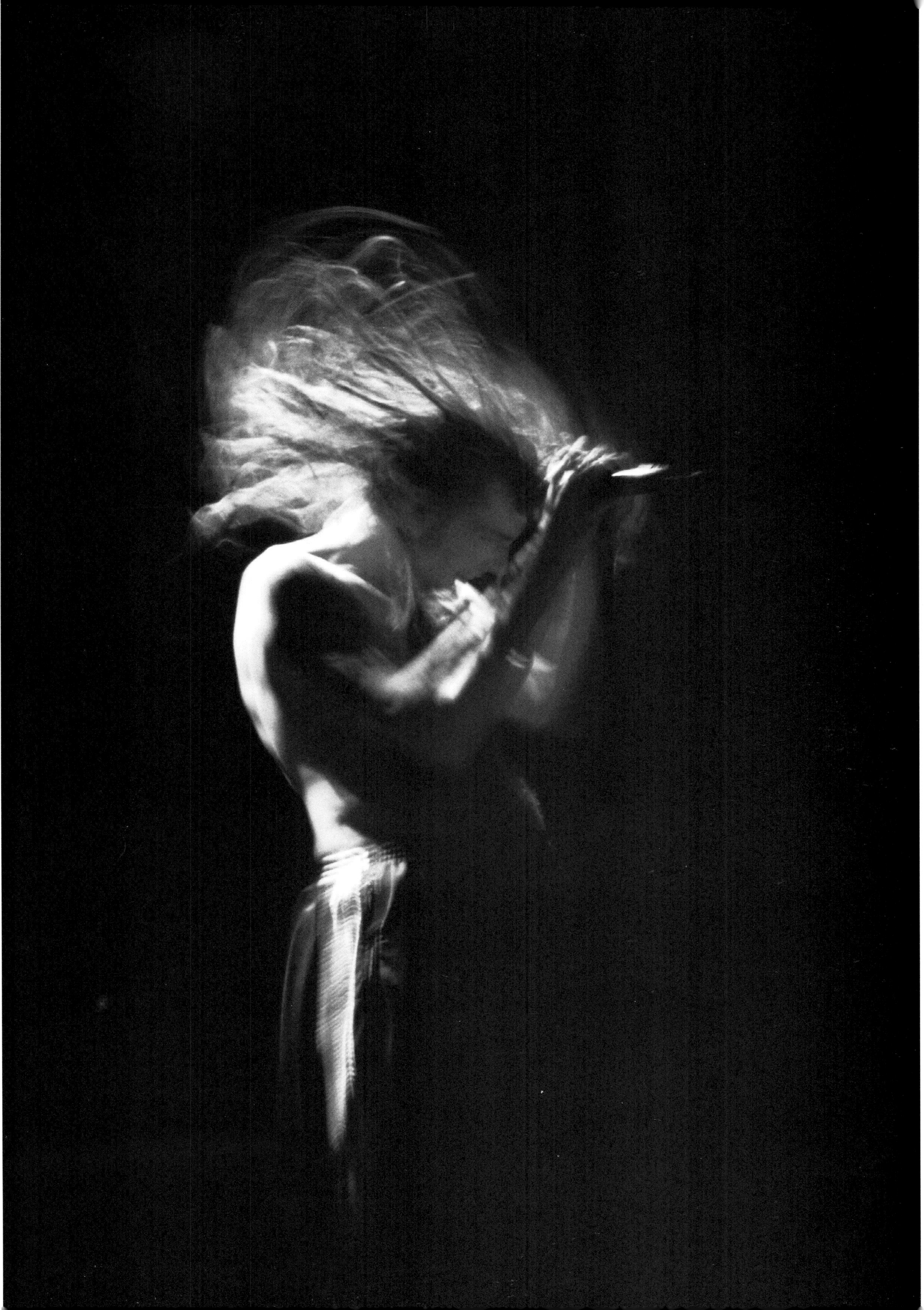

some truly unthinkable stories about dead children, and stated, "I have post-traumatic stress disorder from working there. I go to therapy. That's what they did in Vietnam—all that shit. When you're fucking doing something so heinous that your brain does not know how to register it, you make a joke out of it just to comprehend it. That's the only way you can stay sane. If you take that shit seriously, you'd blow your head off."

In a story about the rising popularity of Korn in the *Los Angeles Times,* on January 19, 1996, Chief Deputy Coroner Jim Matouf, Jonathan's former supervisor, was quoted. "He was reluctant at first," he stated. "When Jonathan came in, he didn't know if he'd be able to handle it. But he got so interested in it, and he became very knowledgeable. We lost a good autopsy assistant there when he left Bakersfield." Alas, another good man lost to rock and roll....

Jonathan's outlook on his time spent dealing in death seems to vary; at times, he admits to having "loved it," calling cutting people open a "rude, sick rush." At other moments, when he discusses it, it is as if he is recalling time spent in hell itself. The conflicting emotions he has are no less powerful for their disparity, and fuel much of the confusion and rage of his music. In a very honest moment, he told *Livewire* in July 1996, "Yes, I know it has an effect on me, being surrounded by death. I have learned to appreciate my life. You have no idea what I see. There are all these bodies brought in, and so many of them are kids. I see people my age mutilated from car wrecks, gang violence, or just being in the wrong place at the wrong time. It's really sad. I was working on all these kids that were my age, and younger. They never got the chance to experience life.... It made me decide to live mine to the fullest. I don't want to waste any time because nothing is promised."

Jonathan Davis' love/hate relationship with his career of choice was not completely satisfying him, and he turned again to music, singing for a local band called SexArt. Ryan Schuck, future Orgy member, played guitar with the band from time to time. SexArt never released an album, but played more than a few local gigs. As fate would have it, Munky and Head were back from L.A. visiting their families in Bakersfield in 1993 and went to a bar to check out the scene. A couple of beers later, they decided to move on and—how's this for drama—they were literally walking out the door when they heard the voice of their future front man. Legend has it that the two looked at each other with their mouths hanging open and turned right back around. This guy had something. He wasn't exactly their style, with his make-up, leopard skin tights, and skirts, but there was a vibe of the strongest kind. They got in touch with him within days and had him over for an audition. "I didn't wanna do it, I went to a psychic. She told me I was stupid if I didn't do it, so I went down and tried out," Jonathan recalls in the *Who Then Now?* video. Before he had even finished singing the first song through the cheap starter-kit microphone, they all knew that they were fated to be a group. This was it.

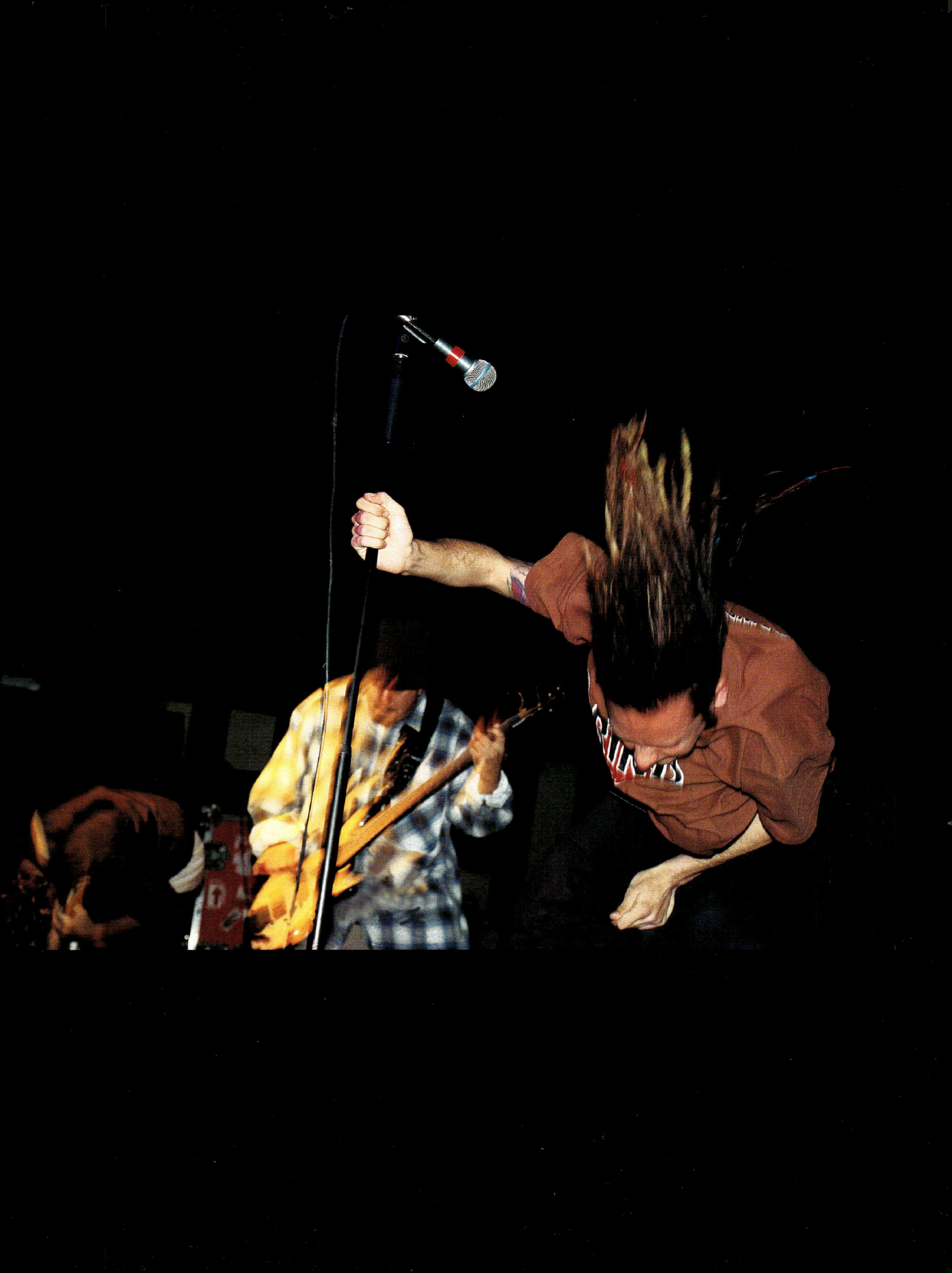

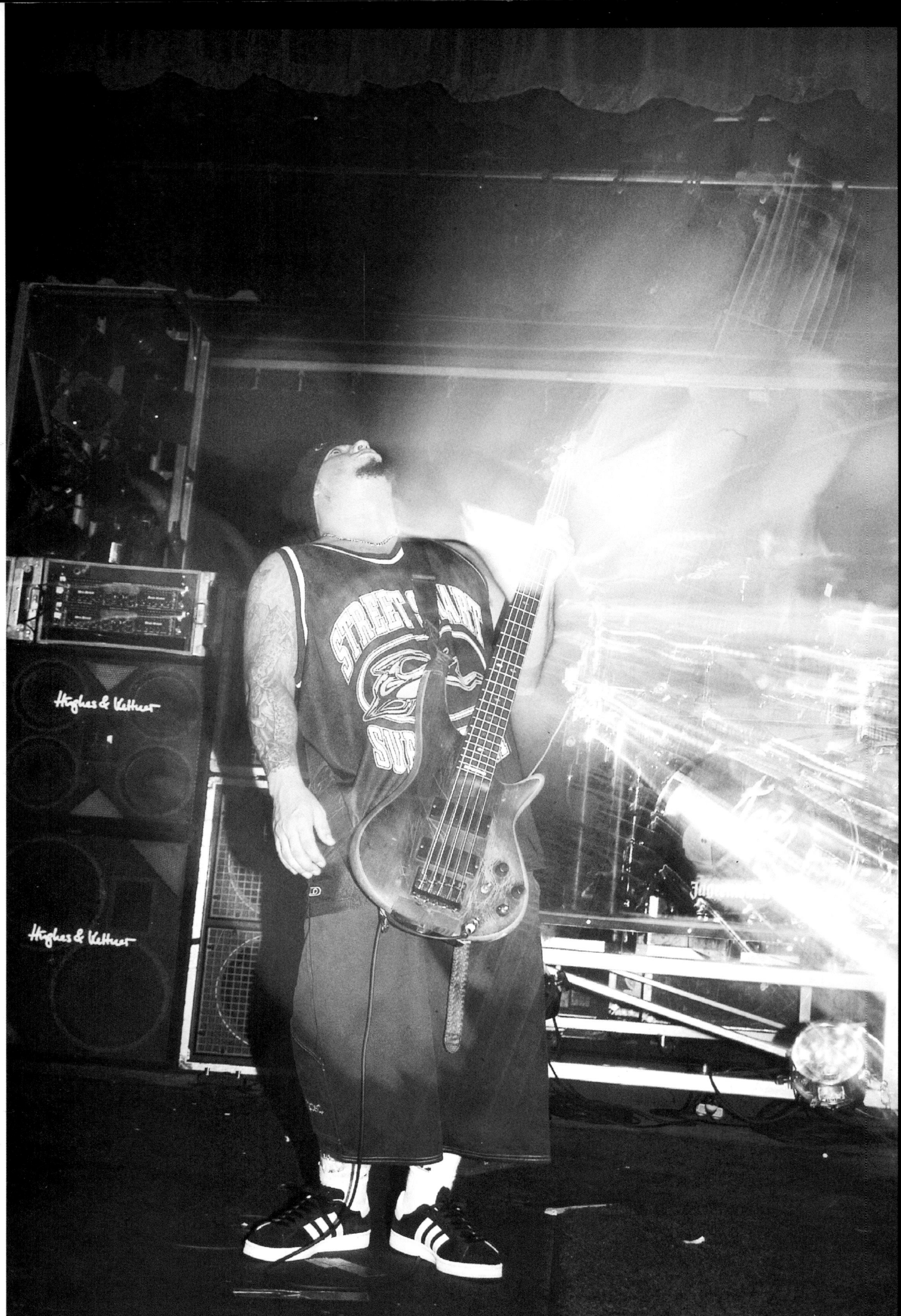
Hughes & Kettner
Hughes & Kettner

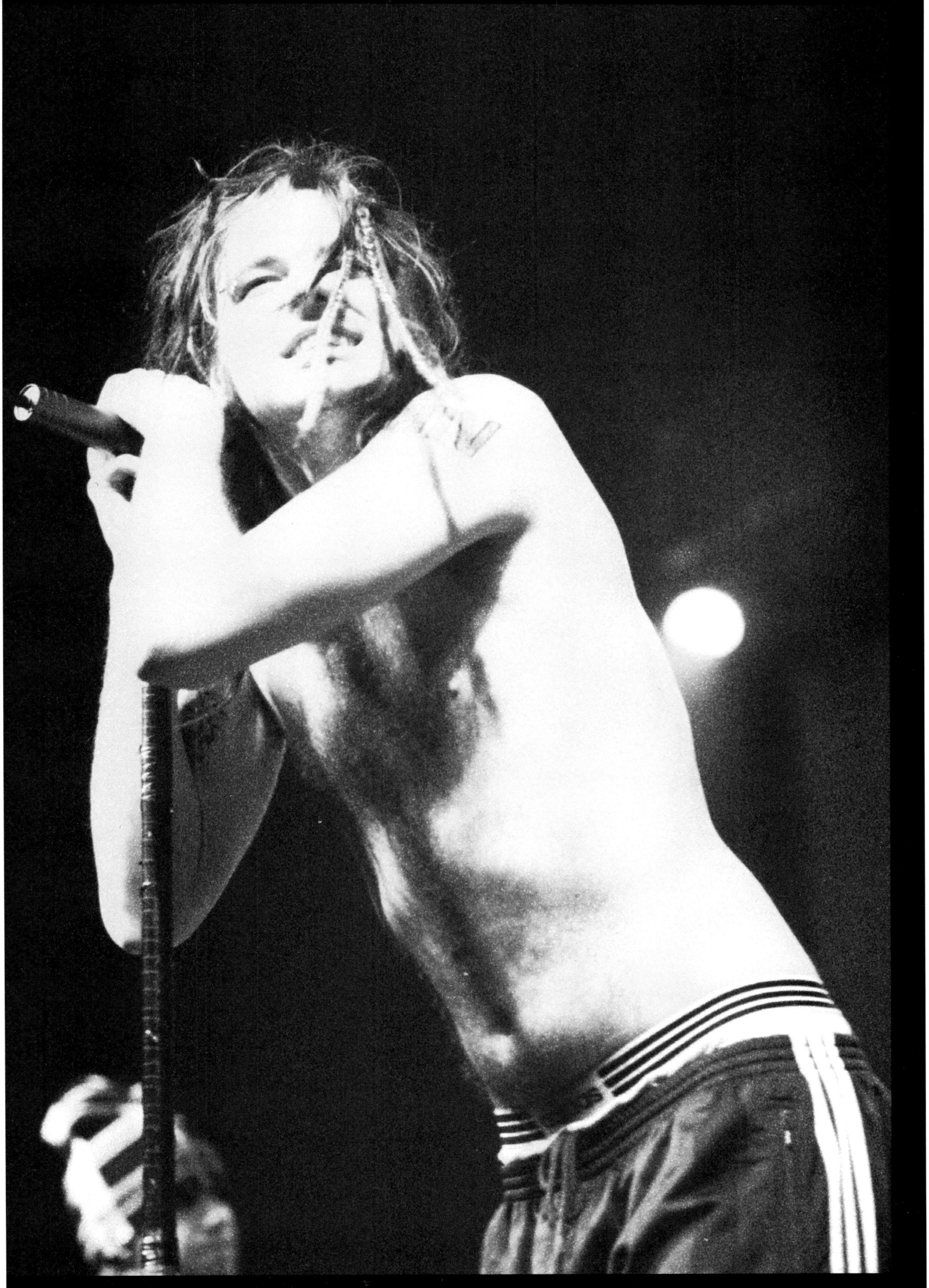

SHOOTS AND LADDERS
AND IMMORTALITY

The diverse musical leanings of all five members came together effortlessly. Their now signature blend of newfangled heavy metal, hip-hop, funk, rock, hardcore, and deep groove was an uncalculated concoction. The band does cite Faith No More as an influence of sorts, mainly, it seems, by the example they set; they were heavy, but they were most definitely not metal. Korn's witch's brew of sound was set to redefine the term.

Once the fivesome got together, they needed a new name. Allegedly Korn just came to Jonathan, and the others, once he spat it out, said, "Fuck, yeah!" Jonathan created the ominous, childlike Korn logo with just one attempt, writing the band's name with his left hand with a crayon. "The music makes the name, because Korn's a dumb name, " David explained on the *Who Then Now?* video. "But once a band gets established, it makes the name cool."

Korn began playing gigs that summer. Their early days on the road were more pain-in-the-ass than sex-drugs-and-rock-and-roll. The future rock stars cruised along in their decidedly unsexy R.V. with an instrument, amp, and drum kit-filled trailer precariously attached to it, driving themselves to their inaugural gigs. As David reminisced to *Metal Hammer* in its February 1996 issue, the trailer "broke down about four times the day we left. We left in L.A., and broke down in San Bernardino!" The band was spotted by Epic/Immortal Records A&R man Paul Pontius at a gig in Huntington Beach, California. Some four years later, he described the unique sound of Korn to *Request* magazine in its October 1998 issue as "the new genre of rock. Metal's passé. It's putting a label on music; their music leans hard, but spans the entire music scene." The group had a few offers on the table, but went with Immortal due to their more hands-off approach. Korn, though a young band, knew enough not to sign away all of their creative freedom.

What was to be *Korn*, the band's debut album that would break the mold wide open, was recorded at Malibu's very rural Indigo Ranch Studios, with additional recording at Bakersfield's Fat Tracks. Of their producer, Ross Robinson, David told *Metal Hammer* in its February 1996 issue, "Ross is a very pure and clean-spirited person, and you feel it when you're with him. He's the kind of person that can draw that out of you." Jonathan added, "I felt very safe with Ross."

Before Korn was released, the band personally passed out flyers at gigs they played for free with Biohazard and House of Pain advertising their forthcoming debut. If the lucky mosher bothered to read, fill out, and send in the questionnaire, he was rewarded with a sample cassette tape of Korn's music. Rumor has it that elusive copies of an alleged demo tape by the baby Korn called *Niedermeyer's Mind* and featuring the first captured, recorded sound of Korn in the form of four tracks ("Blind," "Daddy," "Alive," and "Predictable") are alive and well in Bakersfield, although whose grubby hands are holding the goods is not clear.

Jonathan Davis, never one for understatement, sports a tattoo of one of his nicknames: "HIV." "That tattoo has probably saved my life," he told *Circus* in its August 19, 1997, issue. "You know in situations when passion and lust take over your brain ... I take a look at that tattoo and I remember that the virus is out there and you never know who got it. It saved me quite a few times from doing something very stupid." On the less intense side of name-calling, Head is quite proud of his adopted moniker, which is not, as some suspect, inspired by his outrageous braided do, but rather is due to the simple fact that he has an overly large head. His boastful claim that no hat fits his huge cerebrum has yet to be challenged. As he told *Kerrang!* magazine, "I'm okay with it, though. Big head means I got more brains." Munky is equally proud of his name, which he claims is self-explanatory: he looks like a monkey and will happily display his hand-like feet as proof. Less obvious perhaps is Fieldy, which in fact is a metamorphosis of his original nickname "Gopher" (due to the nut-filled bulge of his

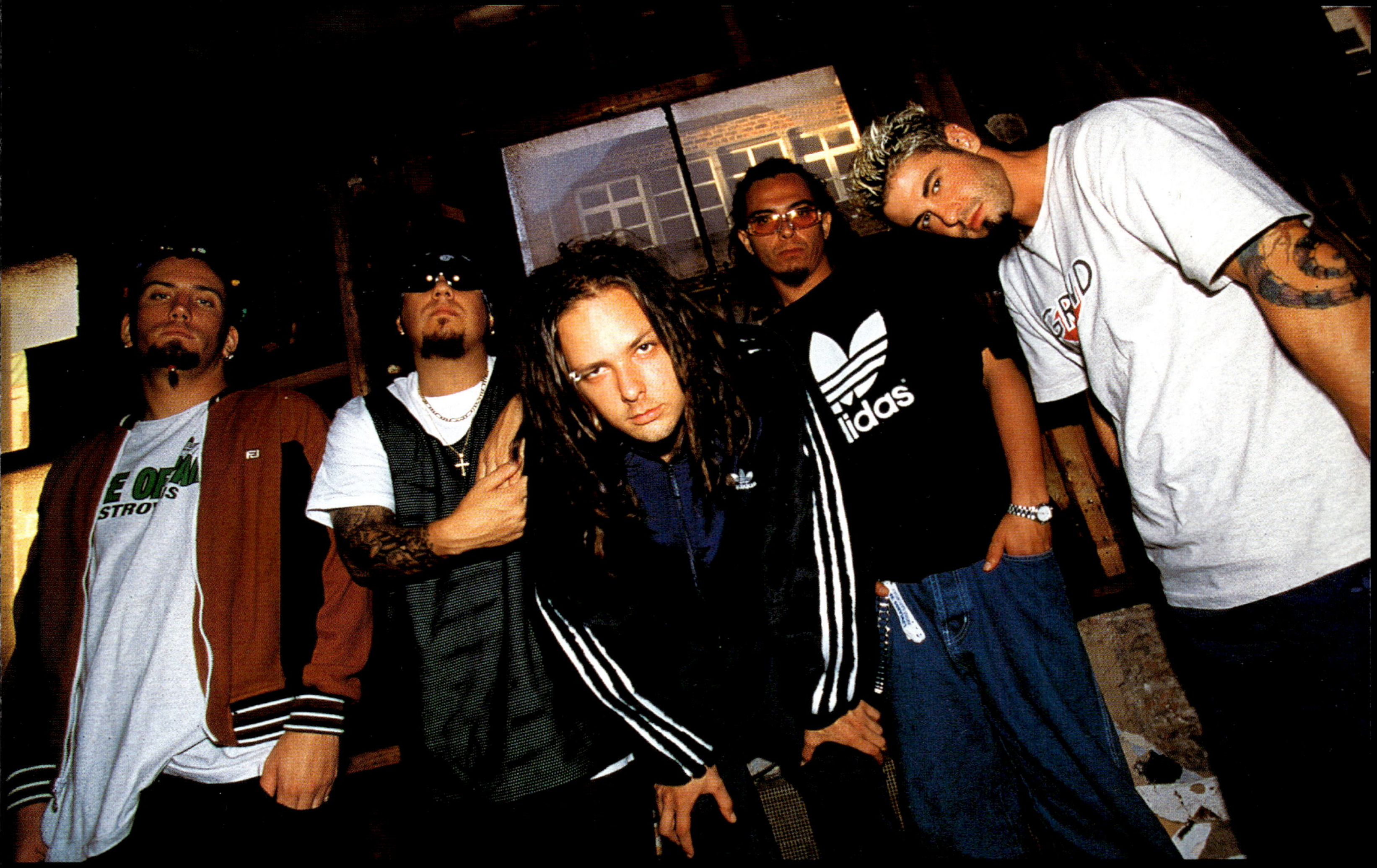

cheeks), which morphed into Garfield, which was of course shortened to Fieldy. The band members seem to nickname anyone they're fond of—one needs only to peruse their liner notes to find evidence in the form of the likes of "Joe 'Bag O Donuts' Shnock," "Coolie," "Vic 'Shut the Fuck Up' Pulskamp," "Michael 'Caco' Villalovos," "Michael 'Chicken' Lamb," and "Graham 'Grim Reaper' Homes," to name a very few.

The band's self-titled debut album was released on October 4, 1994. Little did anyone suspect that years later it would still be on the charts, hailed as the forerunner of a completely new genre of music. The threatening cover artwork presents an image not easily forgotten: a little girl, all prettied up in a purple dress with a matching bow in her blonde hair, brings her swing to a stop in the playground to squint in the sun at the man standing before her. We see only his dark shadow on the ground—he is holding what looks like a horseshoe. The childlike scrawl of "KORN" is also branded in the sandy ground by dark shadow. Interior artwork treats the Korn fan to one of Jonathan's pet dalliances in a scattering of porn mags, the faces of the "covergirls" blanked out with the labels, "Liar," "Whore," and "Bitch." The requisite "Parental Advisory Explicit Lyrics" label makes its star appearance, but is it warning enough?

The listener is introduced to the world of Korn by the dueling riffs of Head and Munky, drawing him into the groove, only to be shaken by Jonathan's introductory growl "ARE YOU READY?" The ensuing mayhem of the twelve-track ride down the Korn highway at three hundred miles an hour is an exhilarating, frightening, and cathartic experience. Of the spat-out vocals on "Ball Tongue," Jonathan told *Metal Hammer* in November 1995, "I don't sing a goddamn word in that song. I couldn't describe what I wanted to do, so that's how it came out. It's a really heavy sound." The album culminates in a track the band has never performed live: "Daddy." Jonathan's out-of-control sobbing, screaming from deep down his anger in howls of rage—"I fucking hate you! You fucking ruined my life!"—is truly difficult to listen to without spiraling into despair. The bizarre inclusion, some fourteen minutes into "Daddy" well after the song has ended, of a taped argument between a man and his wife seemingly over a truck repair manual features such gems as, "You're a hard, hard woman to live with. Oh, you motherfucker, you asshole, you stupid son of a bitch!" It's a bit of twisted levity after the heart-wrenching ordeal of the final track. Any way you slice it, *Korn* is an undeniably ground-breaking debut.

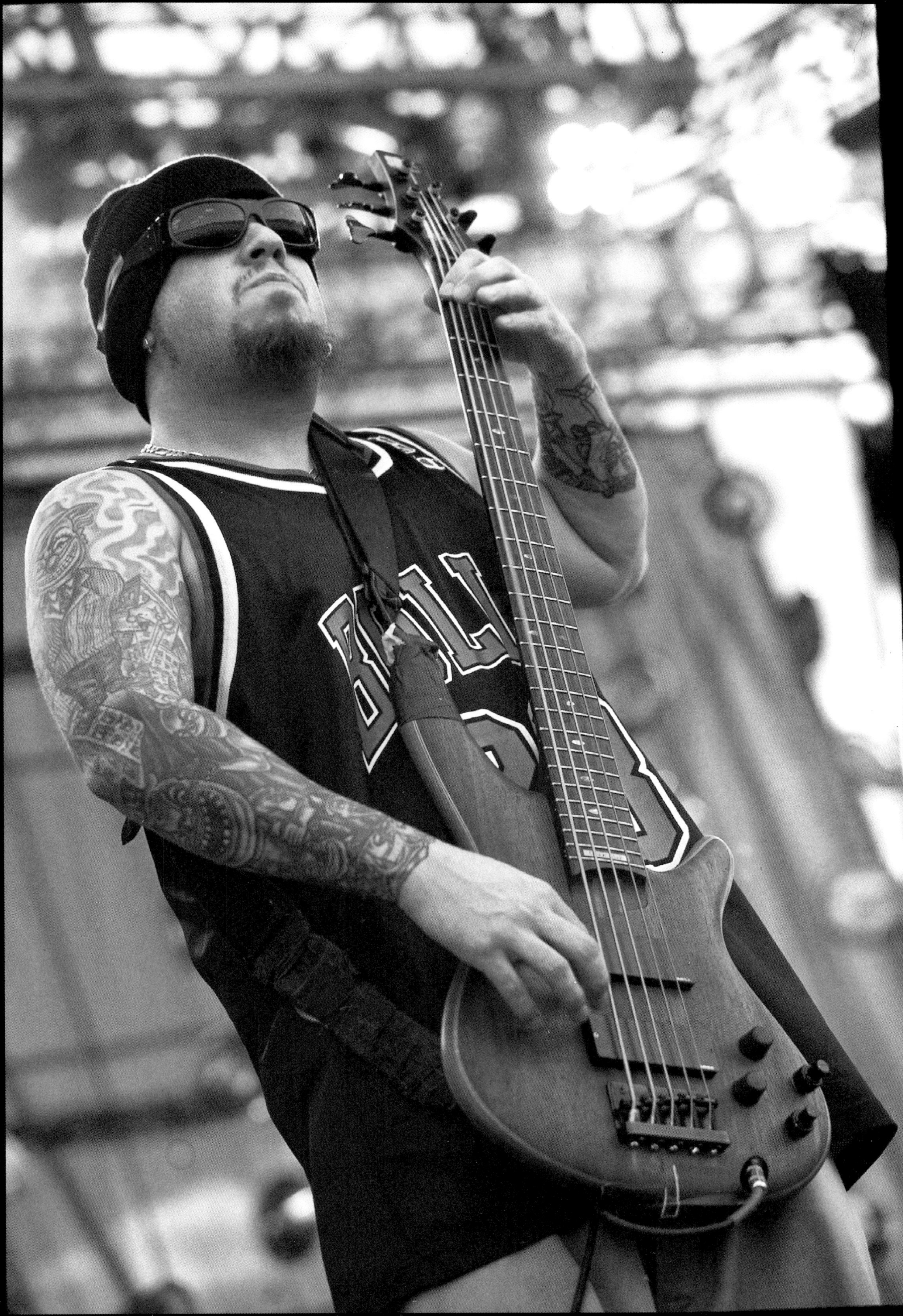

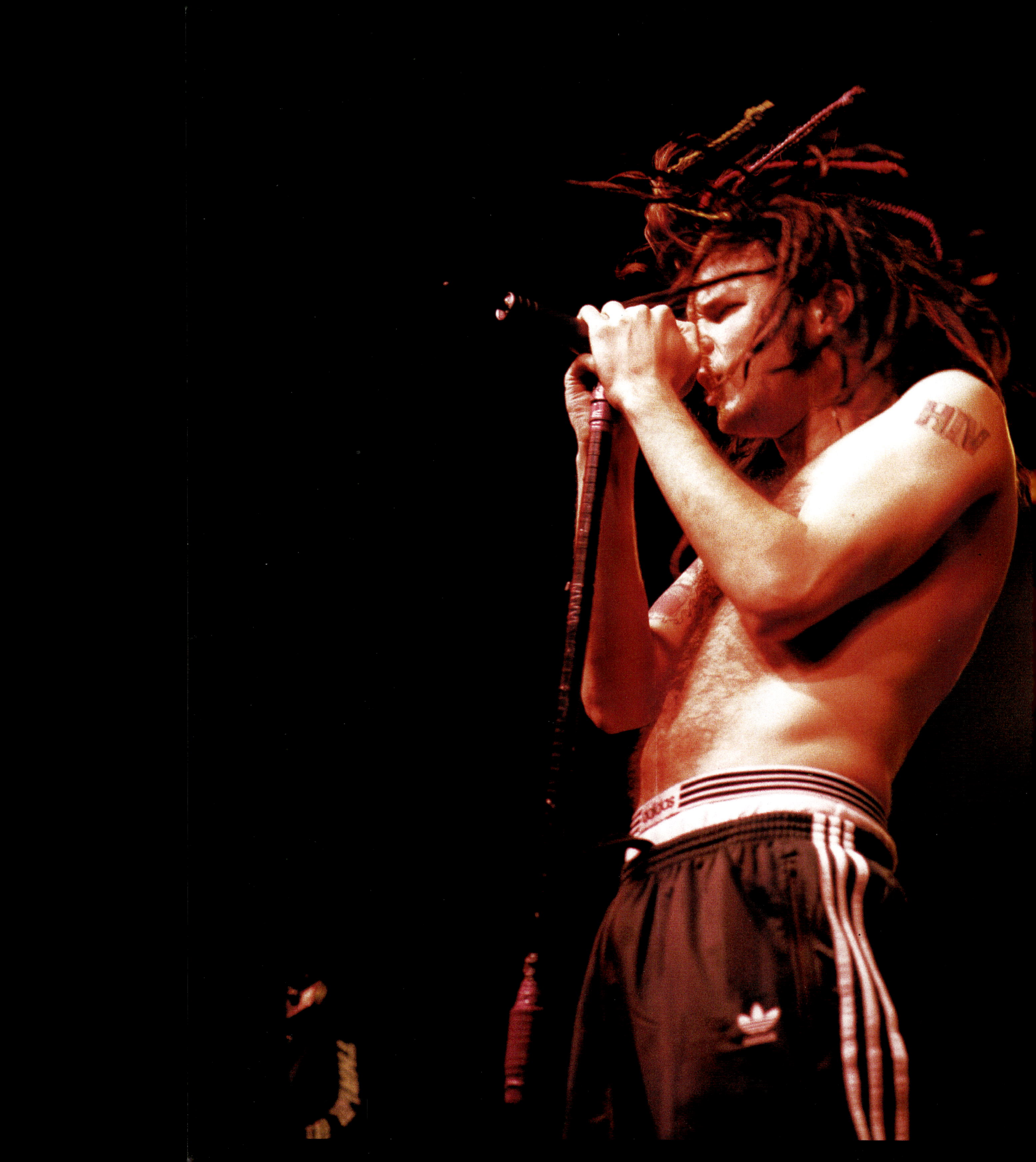
HIV

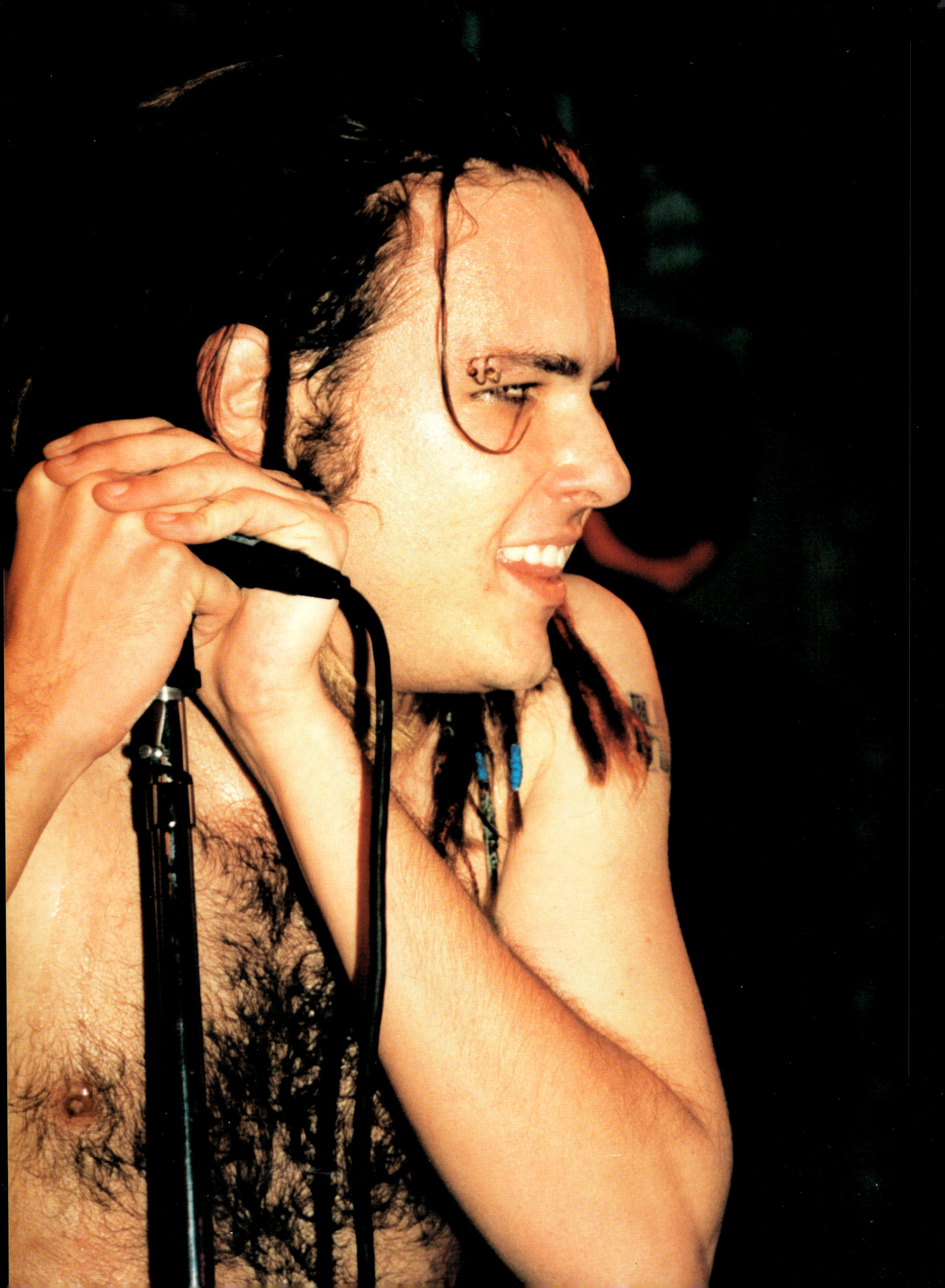

TWISTED AND WICKED

It was not destined that Korn would become the instant "successes" we find shoved down our throats all too often these days. Fame fueled by high-rotation radio play and big time exposure MTV-style were not to be for the Bakersfield five. This was a band that was slated to work their asses off, hone their skills, and build up one of the most faithful followings of recent rock 'n' roll memory. As the band's web-site biography proudly declares, "Korn have earned their success the old-fashioned way through tireless touring, street-level self-promotion, and constant, direct contact with their growing legion of fans. There's no video posturing or fake hype here."

Although MTV only played them on the rare occasion at four o'clock in the morning, Korn made a few videos. A standout is the video for the nursery rhyme-driven "Shoots and Ladders" with it's ring-around-the-rosy, London Bridge cadence. What kind of heavy metal band features a Fischer Price barn in its video? You got me, said MTV. Only Jonathan Davis could give the innocent sing-song of "Knick knack, paddy whack, give a dog a bone, This old man came rolling home" a sinister, terrifying edge. "Clown," a song about a macho fool who tried to hit Jonathan and was subsequently knocked out by Korn's road manager, was also given the full Korn treatment on video. High-school lockers, blonde cheerleaders, and Jonathan huddled on a locker-room shower floor paint a not-so-pretty picture. Things really get ugly when the poor little cheerleader is terrified to discover a KORN tattoo on her back as she pulls her varsity sweater over her head.

As Jonathan told *Rolling Stone* in April 1997, "That's how I deal with my life: by screaming about it. Basically I just want to capture that fucking-pissed-off 13-year-old: 'I'm getting hair on my dick; my voice is dropping.' That period of my life really fucked with me." His philosophy is that for an hour each night he releases all of the aggression and pain inside of him, and he feels that his fans can, through him, exorcise a few of their own demons. As Jonathan rationalized in *Alternative Press*, "It's not a bubble gum world no more, things aren't happy no more. I can understand bands writing bubbly, happy songs back in the fuckin' day when people were getting laid and all kinds of shit was going on. Things are different now, and you're gonna have angry music and angry people."

A history of Jonathan's drug use is a bit difficult to put one's finger on. He alternately seems to have had quite a few nasty habits, and to be afraid to dabble in the alternative universe of mind-altering substances. Methamphetamines have been mentioned. He has often claimed that he spent one entire year of his life awake due to drugs, and, although he realizes the inherent danger in such a lifestyle, bemoans the fact that in his now relatively clean state he wastes so much time sleeping the nights through. He told *Metal Hammer* magazine in October 1996 that "hallucinogenics are great if you got a good trip, but when it's bad it's terrible. I have the biggest fear of losing control of my mind" and carried on to brag about having sex with his girlfriend in their car while he was "all peaked out on speed." Jonathan's excessive lifestyle even caused fans to voice their concerns via *Kerrang!*'s letter page, where worried Korn-devotees wrote in urging the lead singer to look after himself, lest he meet a less-than-happy end. Jonathan is proud to say that when he is at home with his son Nathan, he abstains from partying. Admitting to having come home once in a wasted state, looking the little man in the eyes and feeling unbearable shame, he told *Metal Hammer* in February 1997, "I've never done it since, I can't look at him. I think he saved my life, because the way I was going, I was going to kill myself, dying from drinking." He often admits to drinking as a means of escape from the pressures of fame, but shrugs it off as a necessary evil. He rather candidly told *Alternative Press*, "I'm a wreck. I'm a fuckin' alcoholic; I can't fuckin' do anything without having alcohol in my system to calm me down because I'm so fuckin' stressed about what people think about me." However, he wisely seems to recognize that creativity is often a product, or outlet, of angst, and takes the ying and yang aspects of his life as a rock star and his life at home in stride. As he told *Request*, "I guess I'm happy being miserable. It's good for the art and for you in turn."

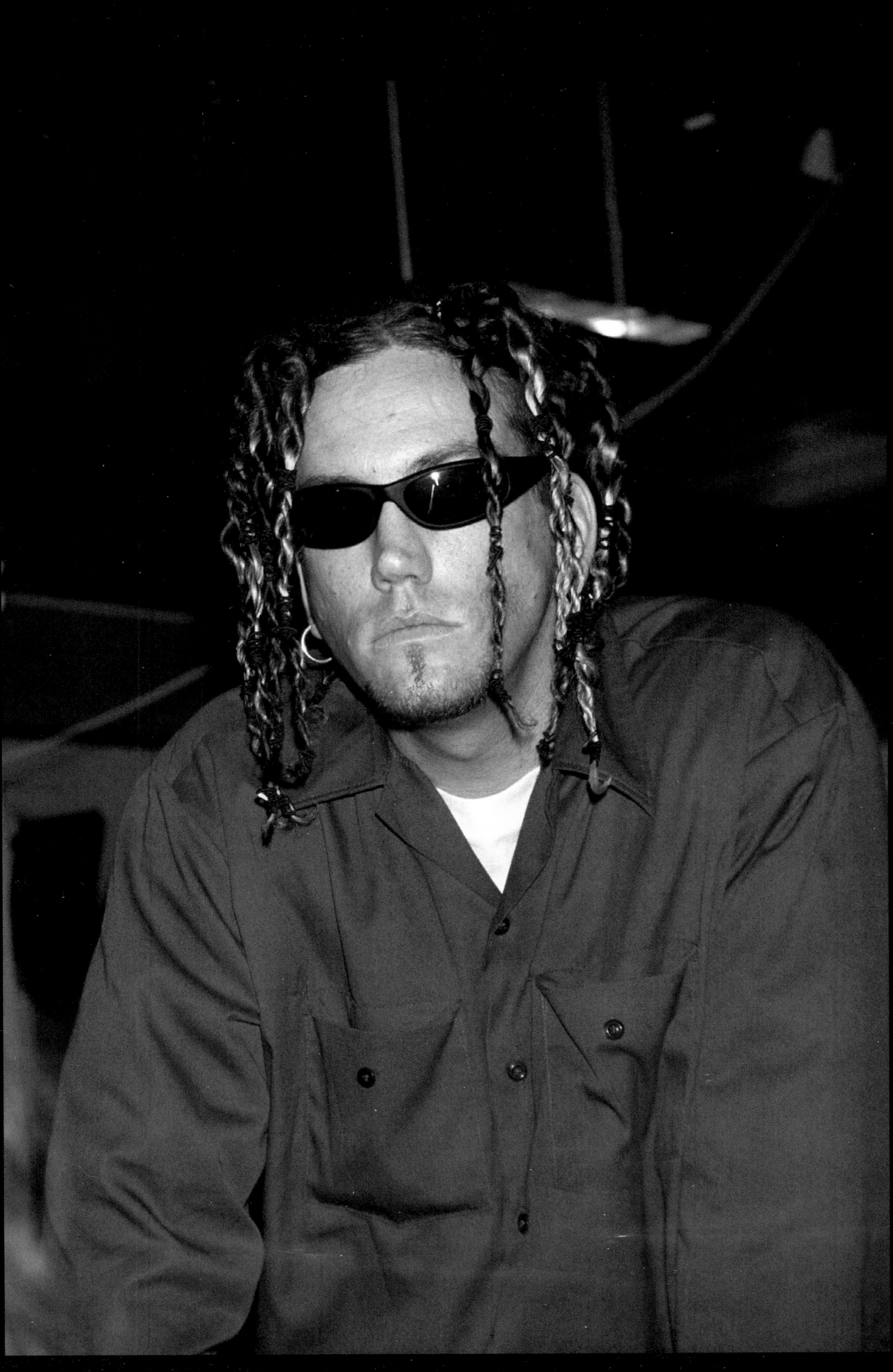

Aside from Jonathan's bout of trouble with Jägermeister (it had to be removed from the band's rider) and his predilection for a Jack and Coke now and again, the band's main vice as a whole seems, amazingly, to be beer. Lots and lots of it. Fieldy claims never to have taken drugs, although has been known to say that Jonathan has driven him to taking sedatives. His poison: brew, and plenty of it, as evidenced in the beer-swilling, fist-fighting, burping, spitting, throwing up, sucking-spilt-beer-off-the-carpet joy ride that is the *Who Then Now?* video. As Fieldy says, "That's all it takes. You wanna go on tour with us, start drinkin'." Head told *Kerrang!* in May 1997, "I don't drink hard alcohol … I just drink beer, and I know when to quit. These other fuckers in the band will drink all night. They wake up with a shitty hangover going, 'Awwwww!,' and I go, 'Why didn't you quit?' In Europe I wake up every day with the worst hangover with that fucking beer. That shit is crazy. It's like double the alcohol, huh? I like American beer because you can drink it all night." David comes across as most concerned with his physical well-being, working out when not on tour to keep his body in tune with the rigorous demands of his career of choice. "On tour I don't like to drink," he told *Kerrang!* in July 1997. "The other guys, if they're tired or if they're not feeling good, they can just stand still for a minute, you know? But I have no choice. My arms have to keep moving. My instrument keeps me being physical all the time, so I don't like to drink, 'cause I don't like to feel bad."

Korn toured relentlessly, gig after gig pounding by without a day off. They played as the support group for a roster of bands including Danzig, Sick of It All, KMFDM, House of Pain, Primus, Fear Factory, Biohazard, Megadeath, Metallica, Life of Agony, Marilyn Manson, 311, Cypress Hill, and Ozzy Osborne. They just wouldn't, or couldn't, stop. The pace took its toll, of course; tales of your run-of-the-mill initiations into the world of rock 'n' roll on the road abound. There were the obligatory frat-brotheresque pranks, like paying their Head of Security $500 to eat a dozen hard-boiled eggs and then throw them back up, or losing a bet with a member of Limp Bizkit that he wouldn't sing a George Michael tune in his birthday suit on stage. While supporting Ozzy Osborne in L.A., Fieldy leapt from a monitor and landed flat on his bass, breaking the instrument and his fall. The crowd, needless to say, was delighted. Jonathan and David allegedly tried to intoxicate rock-runts Silverchair at their Californian acoustic Christmas show, but couldn't sneak the required alcohol past the band members' chaperoning parents. Suffice it to say that the band learned what they needed to learn from their freshman tour experience. And the band went far from unnoticed.

U.K. heavy metal magazine *Metal Hammer* jumped on the Kornwagon right from the start. In its November 1995 issue, the mag likened the U.K. arrival of Korn to the re-formation of the Beatles, and put our five Californian heroes down as "tipped to be bloody huge in '96." The writer went on to say that, "The buzz that surround this band is huge, and when they actually play the audience freaks out big time; the pit goes crazy, even though it's quite possible that less than ten percent of the people here have actually heard the record." Needless to say, lavishing attention on a U.S. band whose album hasn't even been released in the U.K. is not the norm. But neither was Korn.

Indeed, Korn was welcomed with open arms in Europe. At the 1996 Donington Festival, one of Europe's premiere heavy metal gigs, Korn headlined the *Kerrang!* stage, and Jonathan told MTV's Headbangers' Ball VJ Vanessa Warwick that the onstage experience was "incredible. We had no clue. I just went up there and shocked the shit out of me, basically." The band, not strangers to intense shows, seemed truly taken aback at the response they had from the fervent crowd.

The onslaught of Korn onstage is truly a sight to be seen. Jonathan, in his Adidas gear, head shaking, hair flying—his only anchor the mic stand to which he holds on for dear life—is at once the most powerful and the most vulnerable front man out there. Like a stop-action video, his tall frame jerks back and forward to the insistent beat as he holds his head in apparent despair. His charisma lies in his total involvement in the music; rather than performing, he is sharing the experience with the audience, drawing them into his mind and jumping headlong into theirs. As Munky put forth in the *Who Then Now?* video, "There's not one night up there when he's not really feeling his lyrics, and really singing from his heart. Every night. He just, like, sings from his soul. That's hard to find." That much intensity from a lead singer might lead your average band to get down

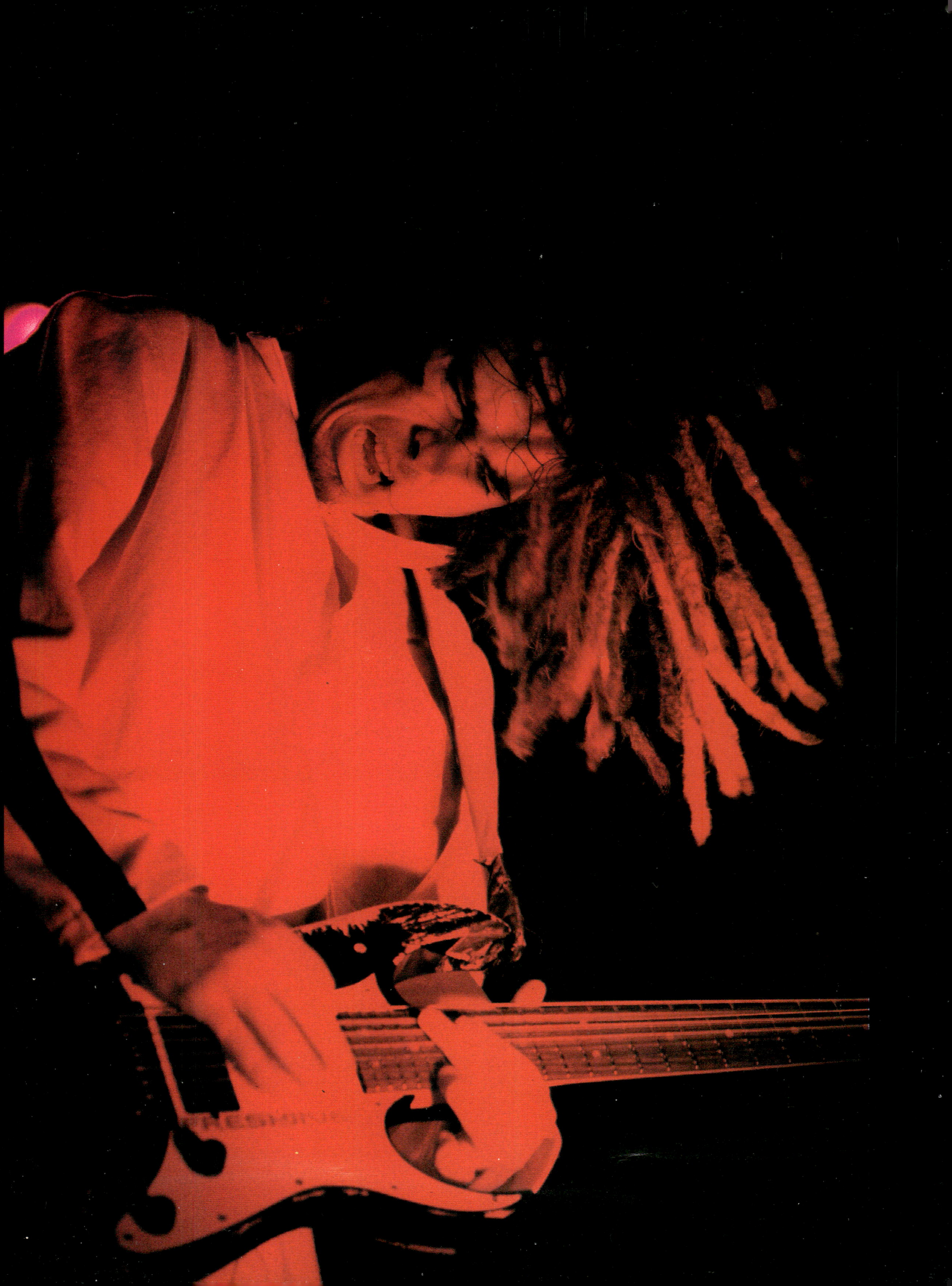

to the business of playing and let the front man claim the stage. But Korn is a unit through and through, and all the members are in it for the all. Fieldy, a self-professed hip-hop head who insists that he never listens to heavy rock or metal, has a style all his own, which refuses to be drowned out by the aural assault of the lethal combination of two of the strongest guitars in the present-day scene, some of the most powerful drumming to hit the stage, and the all-out howling rage of a vocalist the likes of which has never before been heard. Amazingly, Fieldy manages to insert into the maelstrom of sound a distinct and diverse voice. In *Bass Player* magazine's February 1997 issue, Fieldy explained how he creates one of his many standout styles, the percussive clicky effect he deploys. "I either strum all the strings with the back of my fingers, or I grab all four strings at once and pull 'em when I'm slapping," he said, adding that while developing this technique, he tried pulling one string, then two, three ... and "finally, I said 'Fuck it—I'll try all four.' It took practice, but now it's easy." Munky explained the musical relationship between the two guitars and the rest of Korn in *Guitar World*'s October 1998 issue, saying, "Instead of soloing in a traditional manner, we've learned to communicate by creating really raw and emotional sounds using new combinations of textures.... Instead of a solo, our songs have a middle part where the whole band creates a huge, driving groove." Onstage, Munky, Fieldy, and Head simultaneously crack their bodies like whips, pummeling themselves within inches of their lives. Almost more frightening is Munky standing still, upright like a puppet, broken guitar strings on end as he lifelessly performs a hapless Townshend-windmill imitation. David never relents; his precision drumming is at once faultless and absolutely live. In a word, Korn kick.

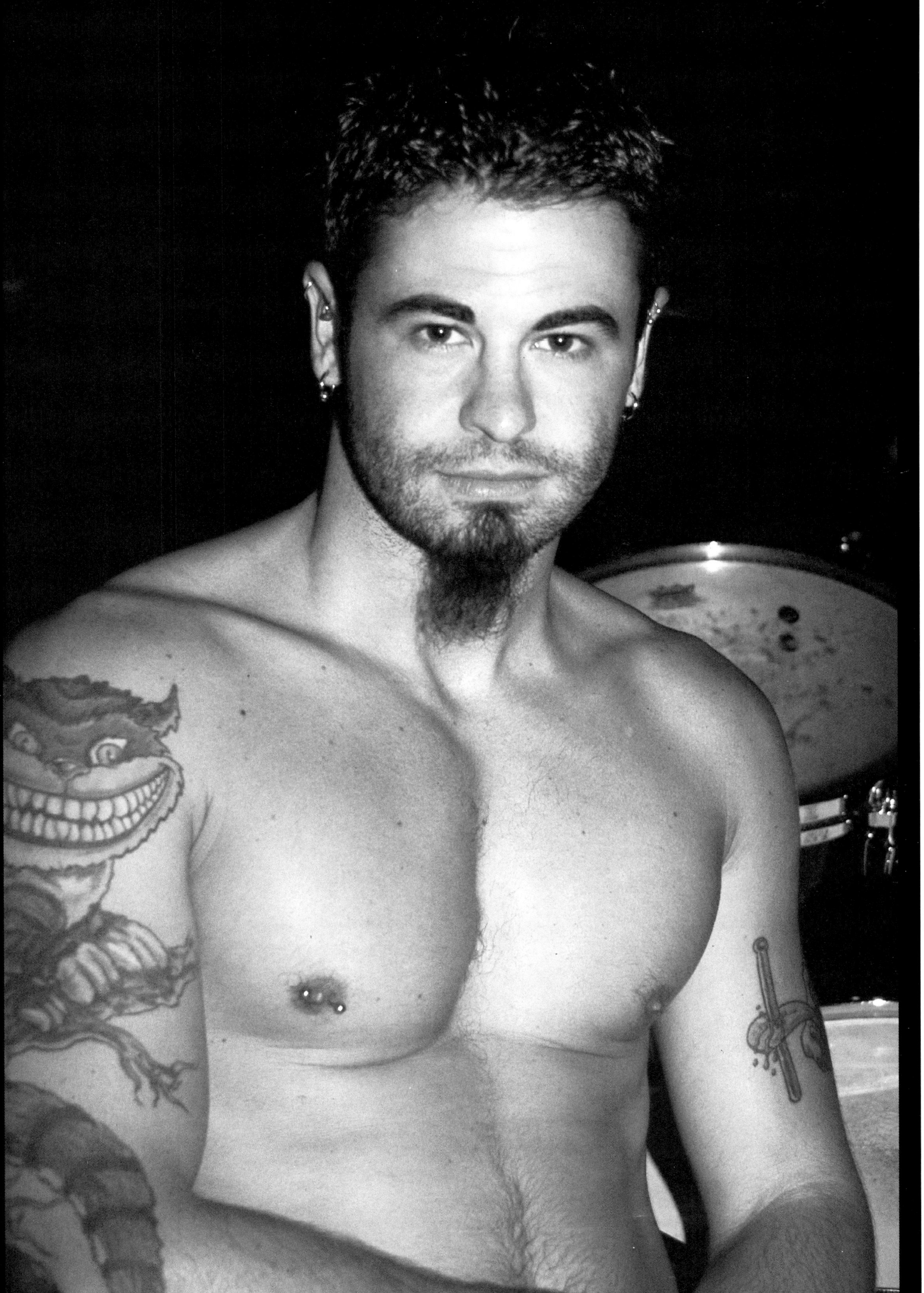

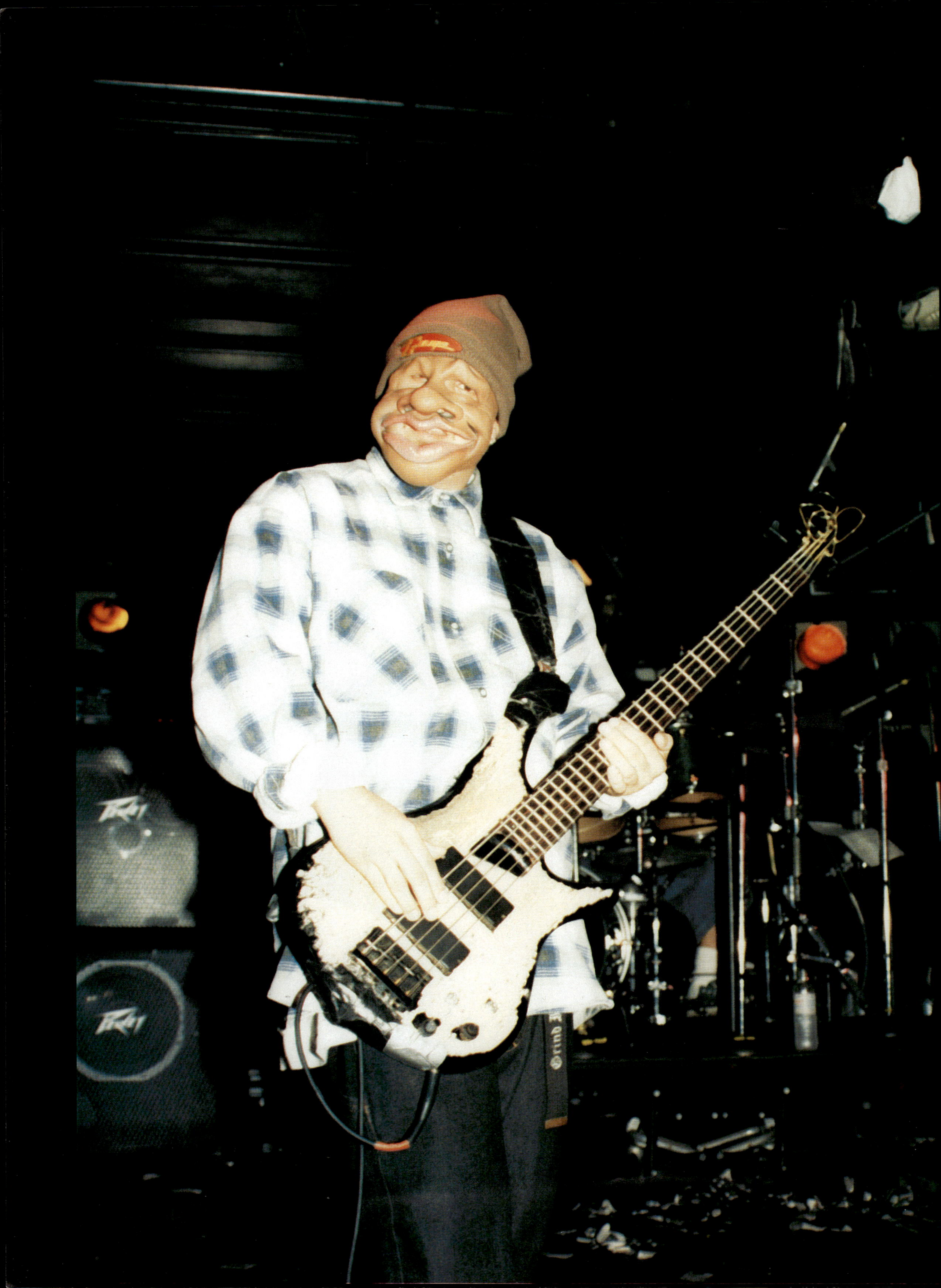

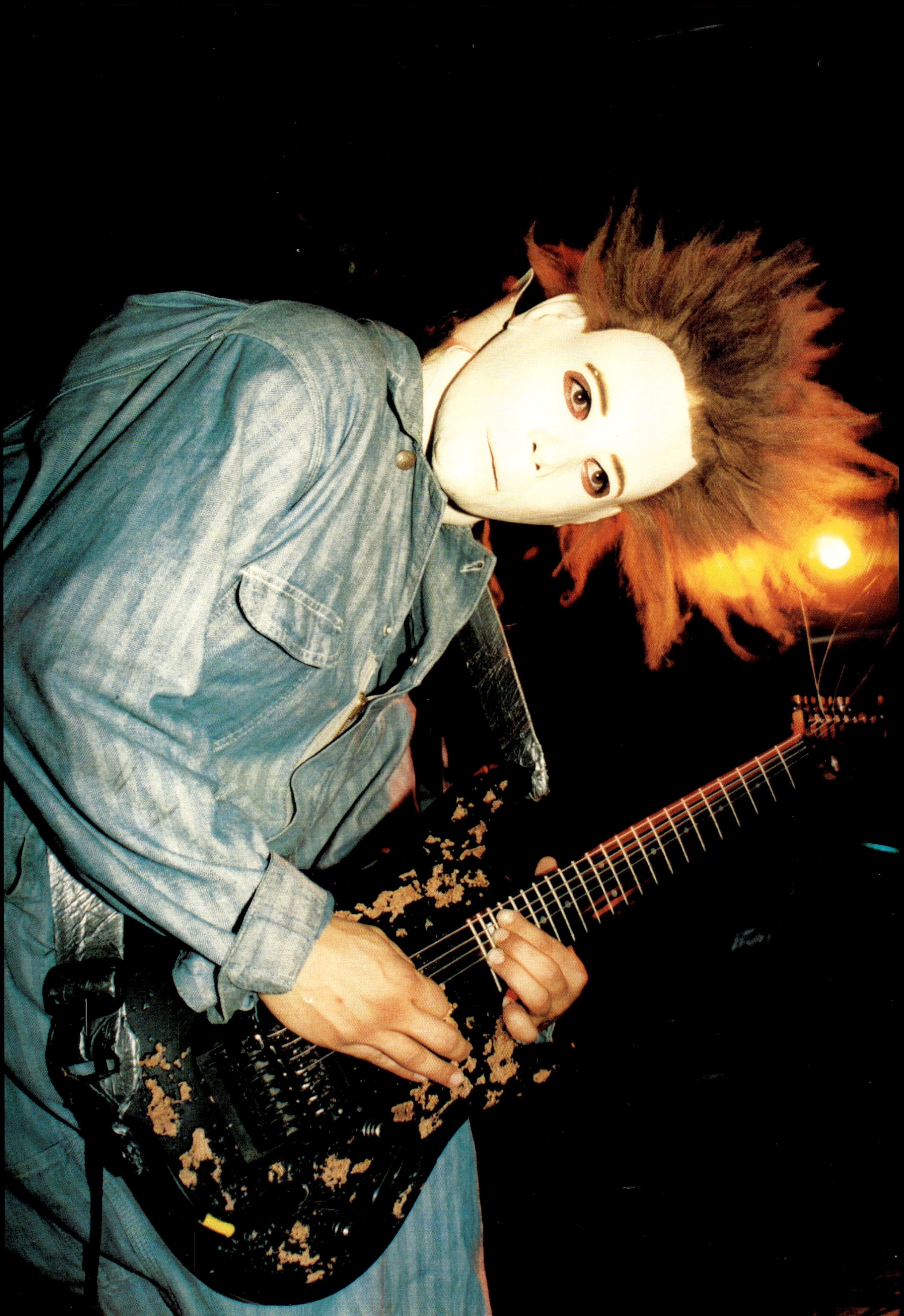

PEACHES AND SCREAM

Korn took a break from the Never Ending Tour not to wind down, but to record their sophomore effort, 1996's *Life Is Peachy*. The album was recorded at a whirlwind pace. As Munky told MAX, a station in New Zealand, in May 1997, "We didn't write nothin' for two years, then we had a lot of creativity build up, like blue balls of creativity. In the studio it just kinda spewed out." The band's songwriting method—a sort of collective building process wherein the four instrumentalists, with the input of Jonathan, develop each other's ideas until they've created a monster—is truly a group effort. Once a song is musically completed, Jonathan composes the lyrics. Thus a complex, multi-layered song can be born of a single riff or beat. "That's how we come up with a lot of the music," David told *Modern Drummer* in April 1997. "Somebody will start playing something and the rest of us will work around it and see where it goes." "Good God" and "Twist" germinated with drumbeats David devised. Jonathan has an unusual recording style: he likes to have as many people as can fit in the studio with him as he lays down the vocals. As band members and studio techs surround the emotional whirling dervish, he exorcises his vocal demons, feeling the need for an audience even offstage. For their new album, Korn stuck with producer Ross Robinson, and returned to live-in Indigo Ranch Studios in Malibu. As Jonathan put it, "Ross is like the big cheerleader of the band. It's all inside of us, but Ross pumps shit up. We both came up together in the music biz, so it's been a cool growing experience. Now he's The Shit as a producer ... and we're doing good."

Although the band has since expressed a certain brand of dissatisfaction with *Life Is Peachy* and its rushed writing and recording, the album certainly has a unique sound, and its merits. At the time of its release, however, Korn were into it, and felt that the rushed aspect of its creation captured a certain fresh, live sound. As David told *Modern Drummer* in April 1997, "we went in really fresh, and we wanted to get it done quickly to capture that energy. So it was probably about 60% knowing what I was going to play and 40% just playing whatever came to mind at that moment.... It ended up really good, and it has a kind of energy I probably wouldn't have gotten if I'd worked everything out beforehand."

Life is Peachy, a sophomore album from a band no one had ever heard of, was released on October 15, 1996, and debuted at a walloping Number Three on the Billboard charts. Fieldy told *Kerrang!* magazine in their March 2, 1997, issue, "I cry over anything, man. I don't care. When they told us *Life Is Peachy* debuted at number three on the charts, I just started crying. I cry over the stupidest shit. I can watch *The Lion King* and cry!" adding, in his usual goofy sense of humor, "It's fun, cleans your eyes out." The jury is still out on whether or not *Life is Peachy* is fun. The somber cover artwork continued the threatened child theme depicted on *Korn*'s cover, this time with a young boy. The black and white scene is of a little boy, hair combed, straightening his tie in a gilt mirror; behind him looms a larger, shadowed presence. Korn's on-line bio claims that "The album title was taken from a kids' popular notebook doodling on the omnipresent yellow Pee-Chee folders: 'Life is peachy but sex is an all-season sport.'"

Jonathan's defense of his vehement refusal to put out printed lyrics with the band's albums is that fans shouldn't rely on the crutch of words on paper. He puts forth the concept that if a fan buys a new CD, and sits listening to it while reading along with the lyrics, the fan is limiting his experience of the music. As Davis told MTV's Serena Altschul, "I think music is something that every individual has their own meaning to the song. They can come up with whatever the hell I'm saying and that's the beauty of it and that's what I wanna keep there." His answer to fans crying out for lyrics? "Stop being so lazy and just listen. They're right there."

Korn is not for everyone, and the album didn't garner much mainstream praise. *New York Press*'s review declared that the album "is to rock music what Linda Lovelace bestiality loops were to film: A premiere example of self-degradation, a masterful response to the seemingly insatiable desire for humans to witness distasteful spectacle."

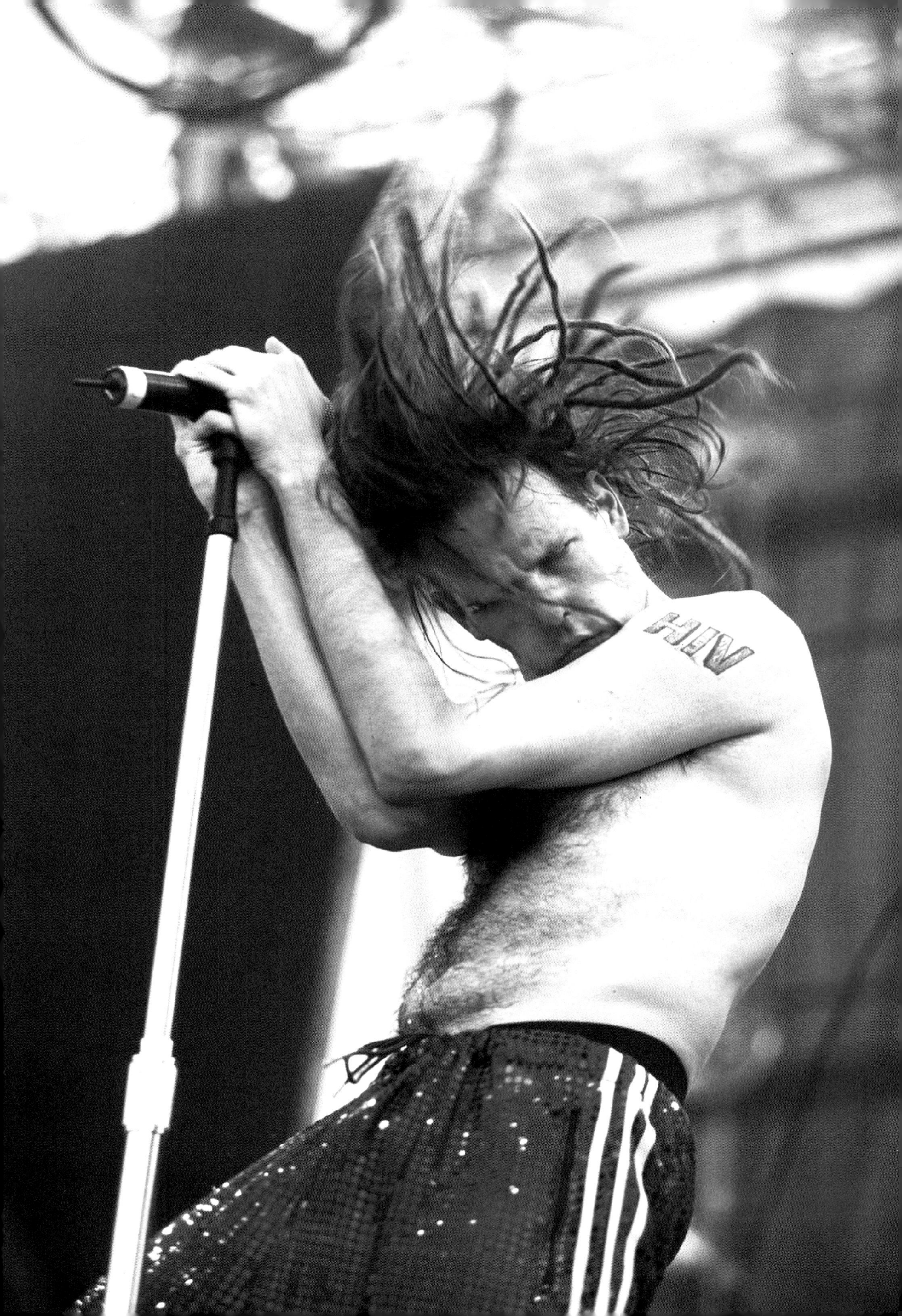
HIV

The opening track, "Twist," is no gentle lead-in. Jumping headlong into the fray, Jonathan's voice, spitting out the twisted rantings of a madman, is a fitting introduction to the delirious, deranged din of the thirteen tracks that follow. Fieldy's explanation in *Alternative Press* of the motivation behind the infamous "K@#Ø%" was that "When you were a kid and you heard the F-word in a song, you'd rewind it 100 times just to hear them say it. So we said, 'Let's put as many cuss words in one song as we could possibly do.' And I guarantee, little kids that are fuckin' ten years old are freaking out on that song. They're going crazy." The single "No Place to Hide" was to earn the band a Grammy nomination, and remains one of the band's favorite songs from the album. "A.D.I.D.A.S." (in honor of both the gear and the like, totally cool schooldays acronym "All Day I Dream About Sex") was another standout tune, with its own video, which was actually granted a bit of that oh-so-valuable airtime. In deference to Jonathan's days in the morgue, the morbid, body-bag imagery of the video surfaced on MTV's U.K. and U.S. airwaves; it depicts a horrific car accident, which results in all five band members ending up on mortuary slabs.

Jonathan Davis's "thank yous" on *Life Is Peachy*'s liner notes begin with "My son Nathan." Jonathan's girlfriend Renee gave birth to a baby boy on October 18, 1995; they named him Nathaniel Houseman Davis. After Jonathan had a dream that they would have a little girl, the couple planned to name the baby Salaam Dementia if it was indeed a daughter. Although not even a year old, "Baby Nathan" is credited with "additional vocals" on "A.D.I.D.A.S." "I love my girlfriend now, because I trust her and she's been with me since I was nothing," Jonathan told *Metal Hammer* in February 1997. "She lived with me in a fucking closet in my house, she borrowed money from her parents to keep me and pay our rent, she believed in me." On fatherhood, in *Alternative Press*'s September 1997 issue, Jonathan declared that having a child is "the single most awesome experience you'll ever have in your entire life. You made a little fuckin' human being that you look at and see yourself in. Having a son is probably the best thing that ever happened to me."

Munky thanks "everyone that helped support Korn this means you, the Fans!" This is a band that never neglects to mention their fans, and truly appreciate every last one of them. In fact, they don't hesitate to shower praise and gratitude on any part of the Korn team; as Jonathan enthused to *Metal Hammer* in February 1996, "Our managers are as psycho in the office as we are on stage! They're so excited and gung-ho!" The lead singer regularly spends hours on end chatting to Korn lovers online, his only complaint being that his two-finger typing speed slows the conversations down. Fieldy told *Kerrang!*'s February 15, 1997, issue, "You get people coming up to you who know more about Korn than I know, and I'm in the damn band! It's crazy. We always think about what it would be like if we were in the fan's position. It takes so much just to go up to us—it's already intimidating to go up to a band—and then if you're going to be a dick to those kids, it's fucked. They're working their way up to you and they finally get talking to you, so just be cool, you know? They're just people and we're just people."

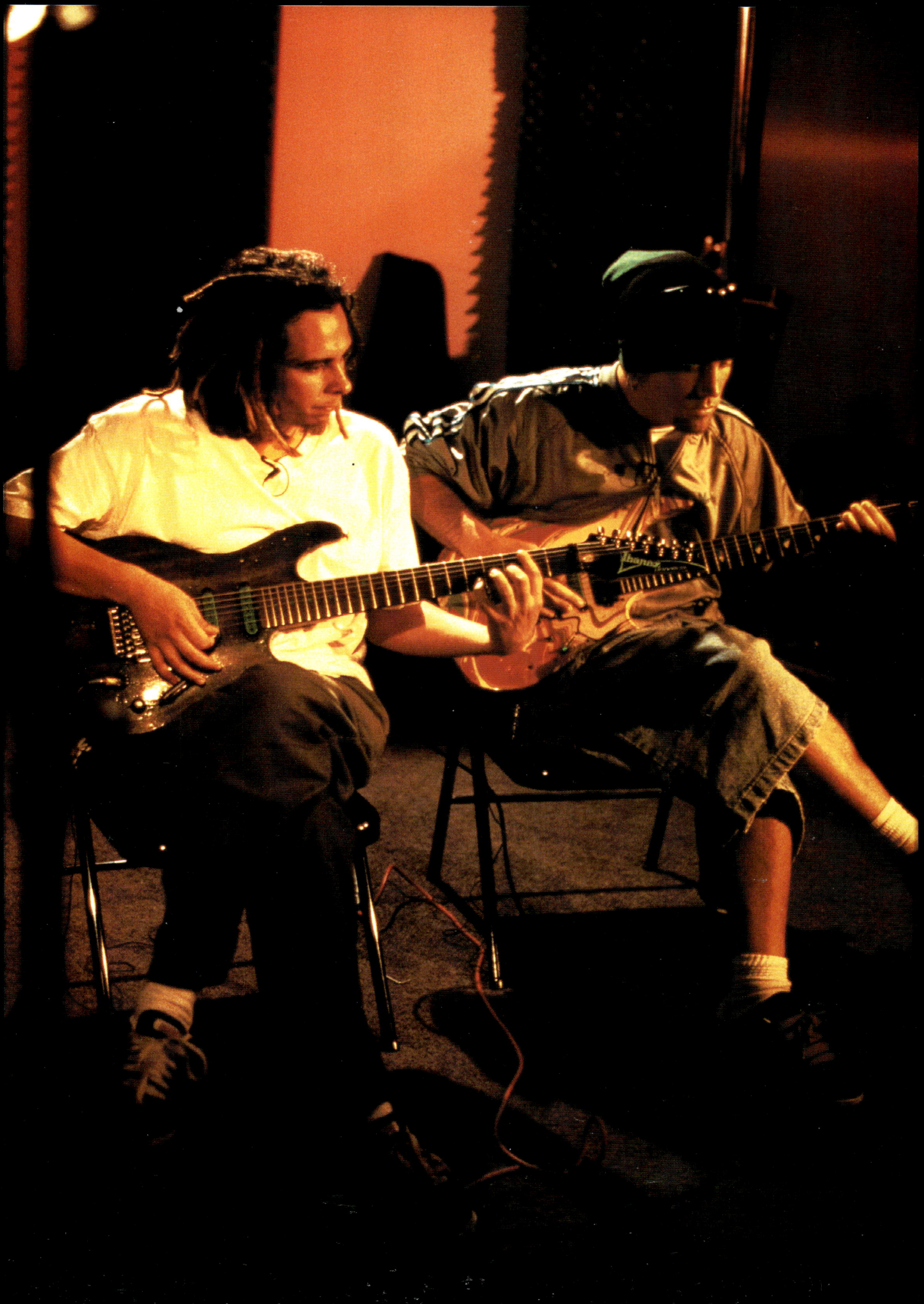

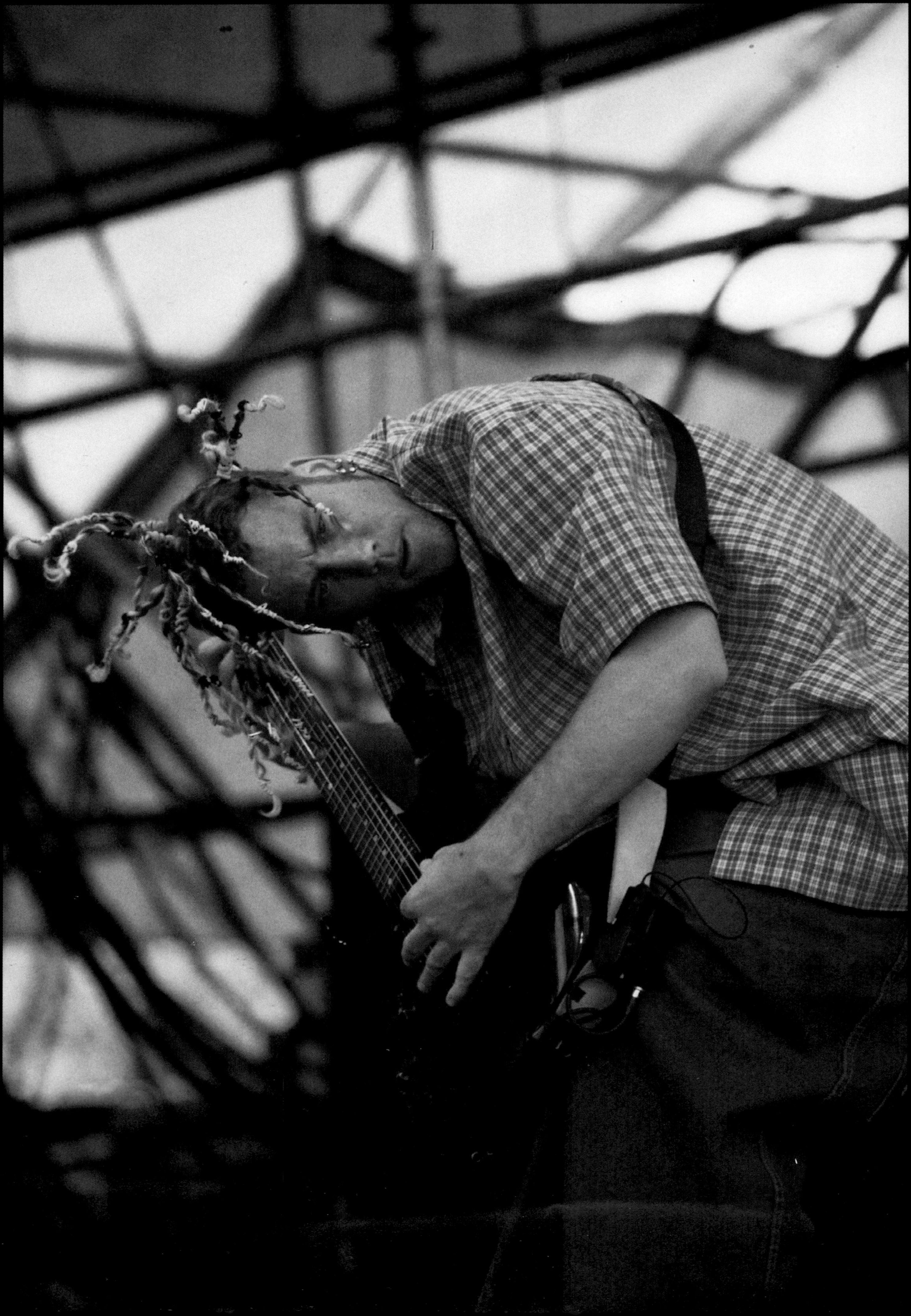

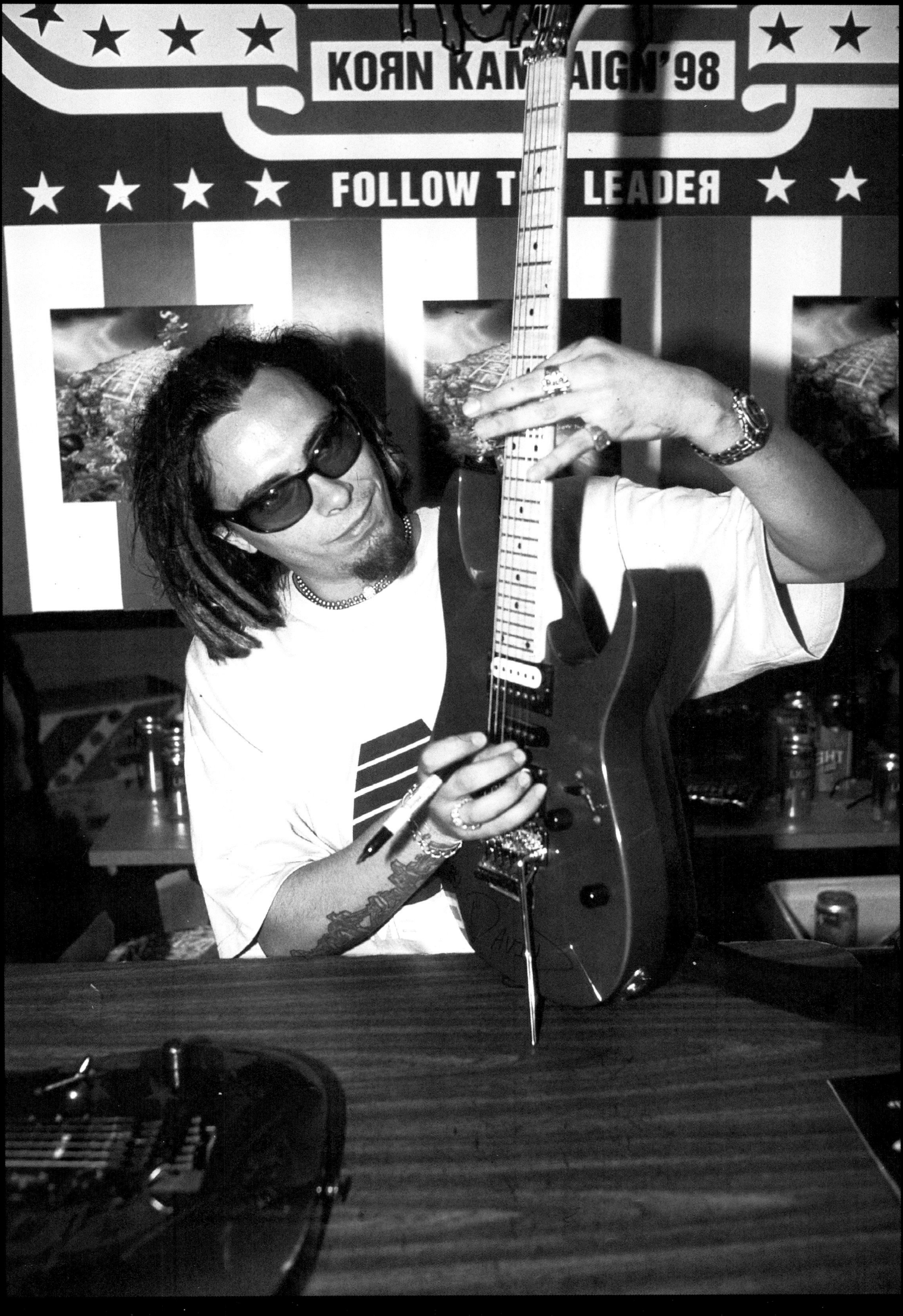
KORN KAM AIGN'98
FOLLOW T LEADER

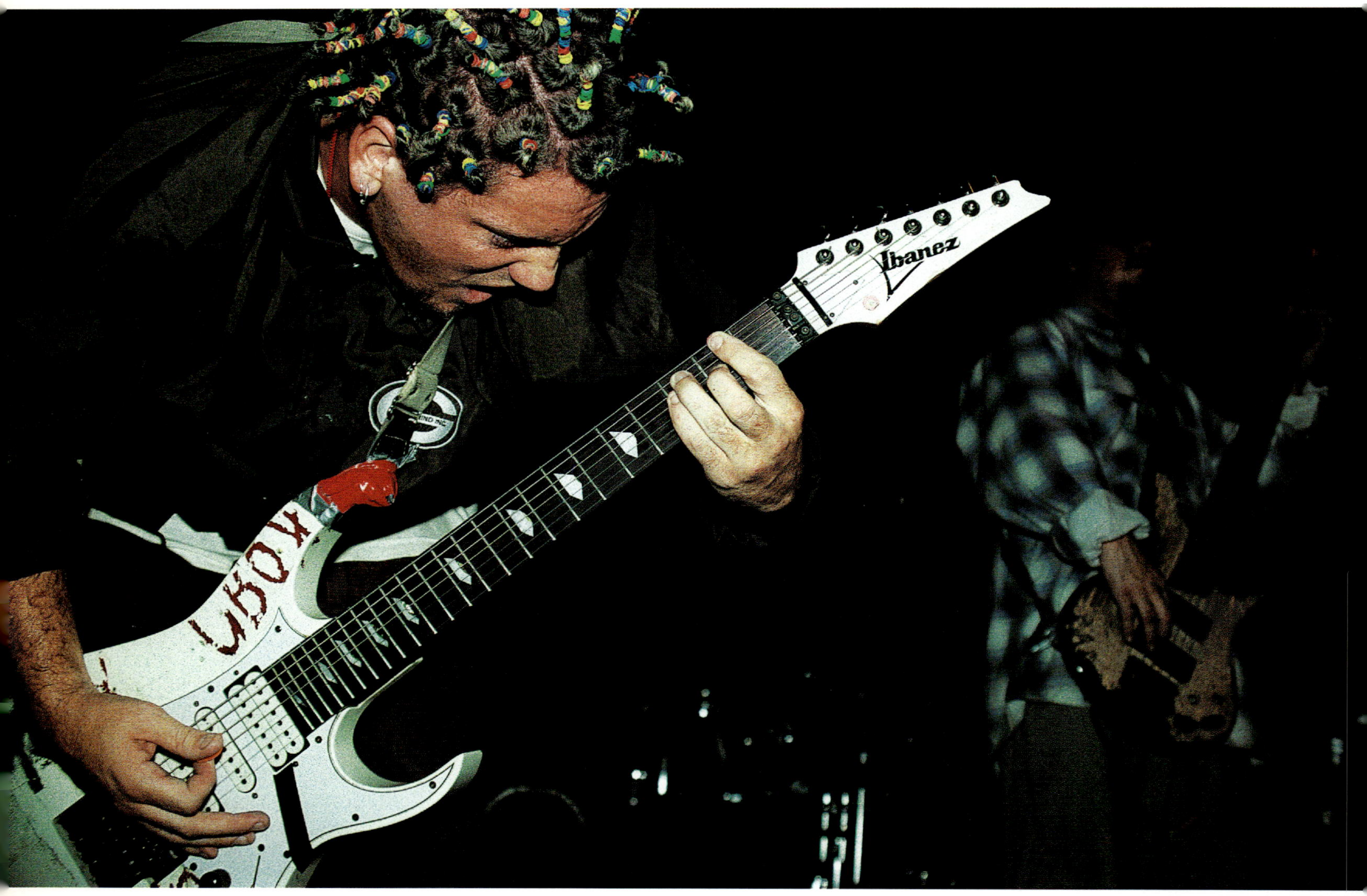
Ibanez

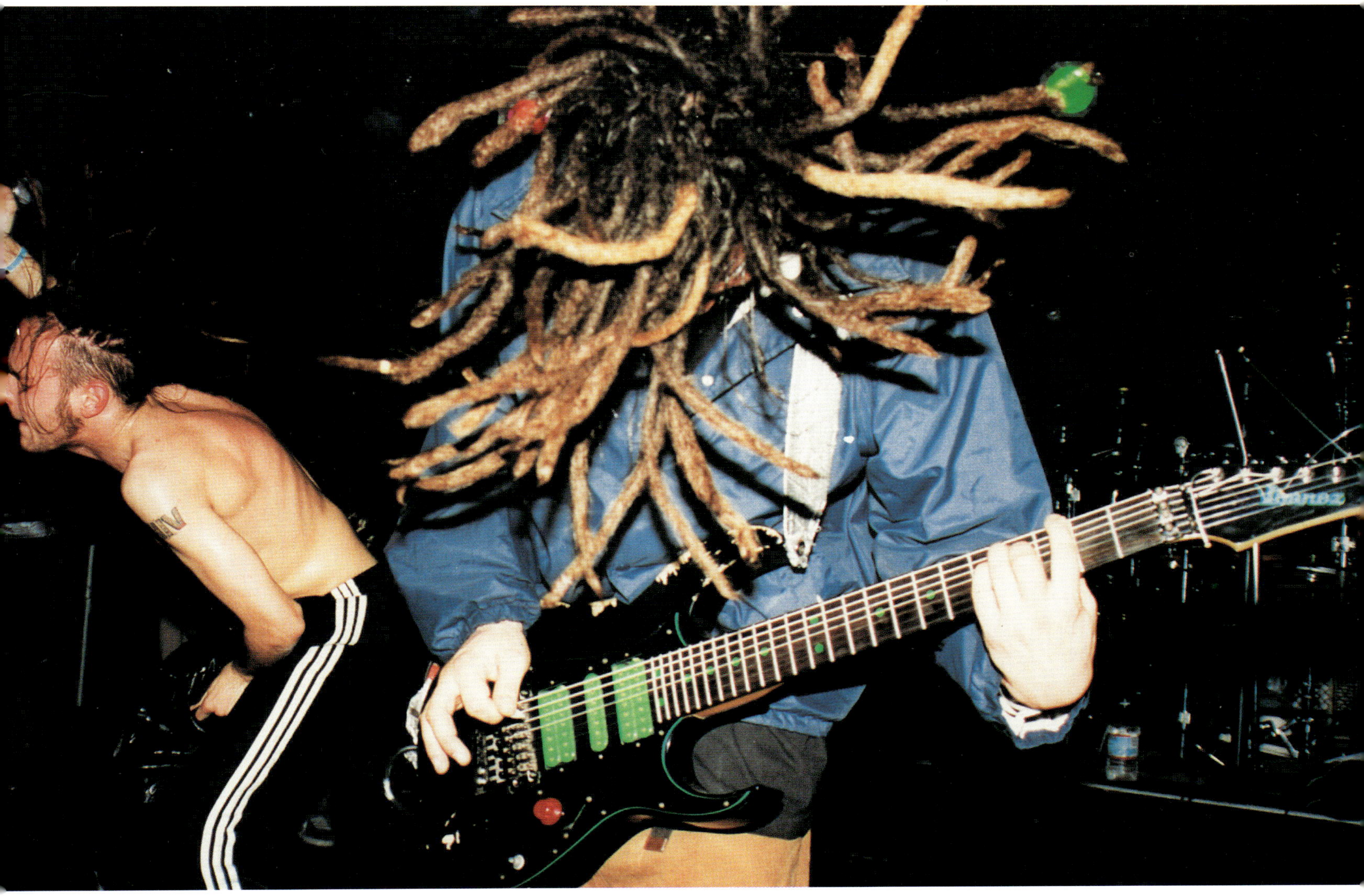

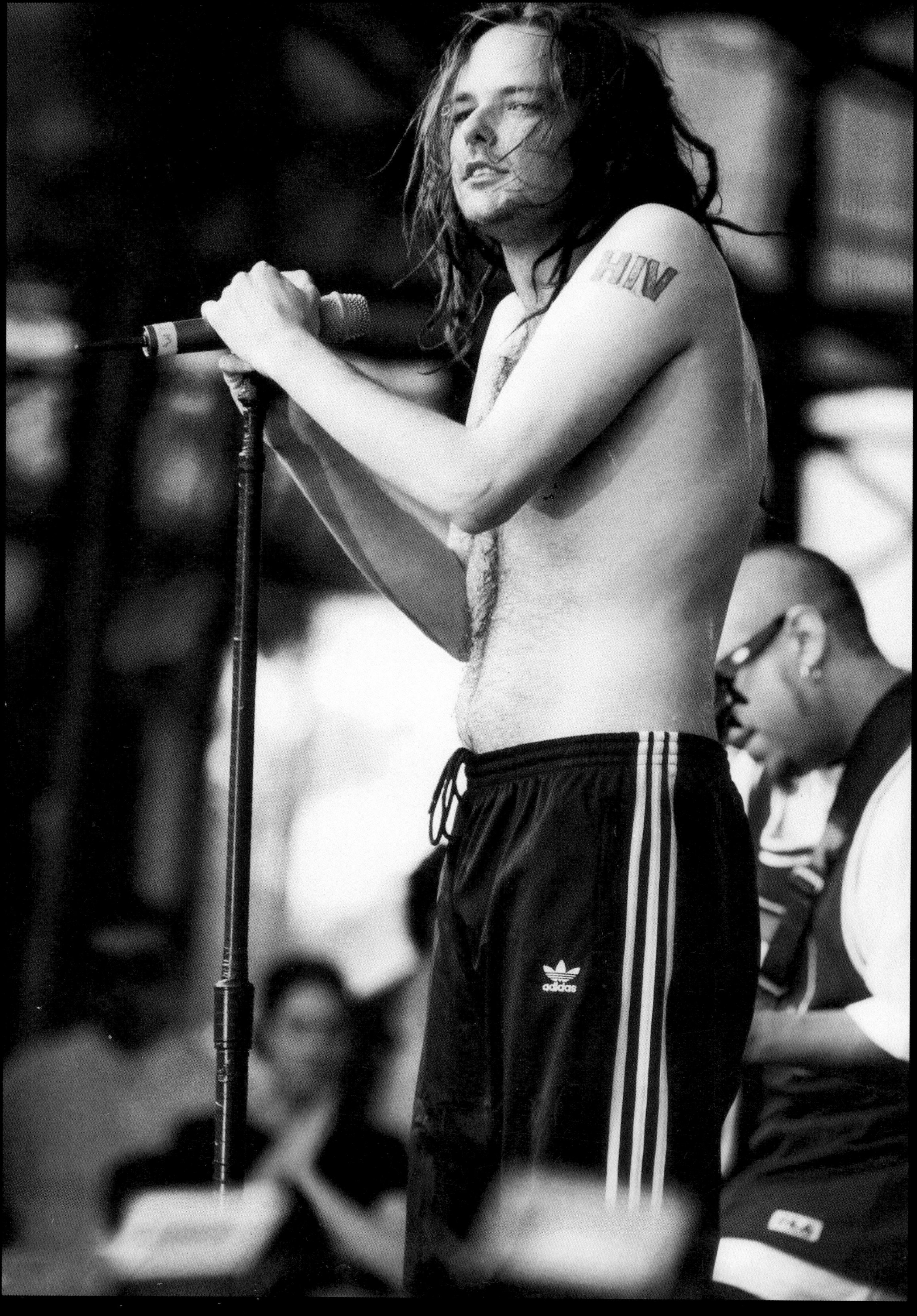
HIV
adidas

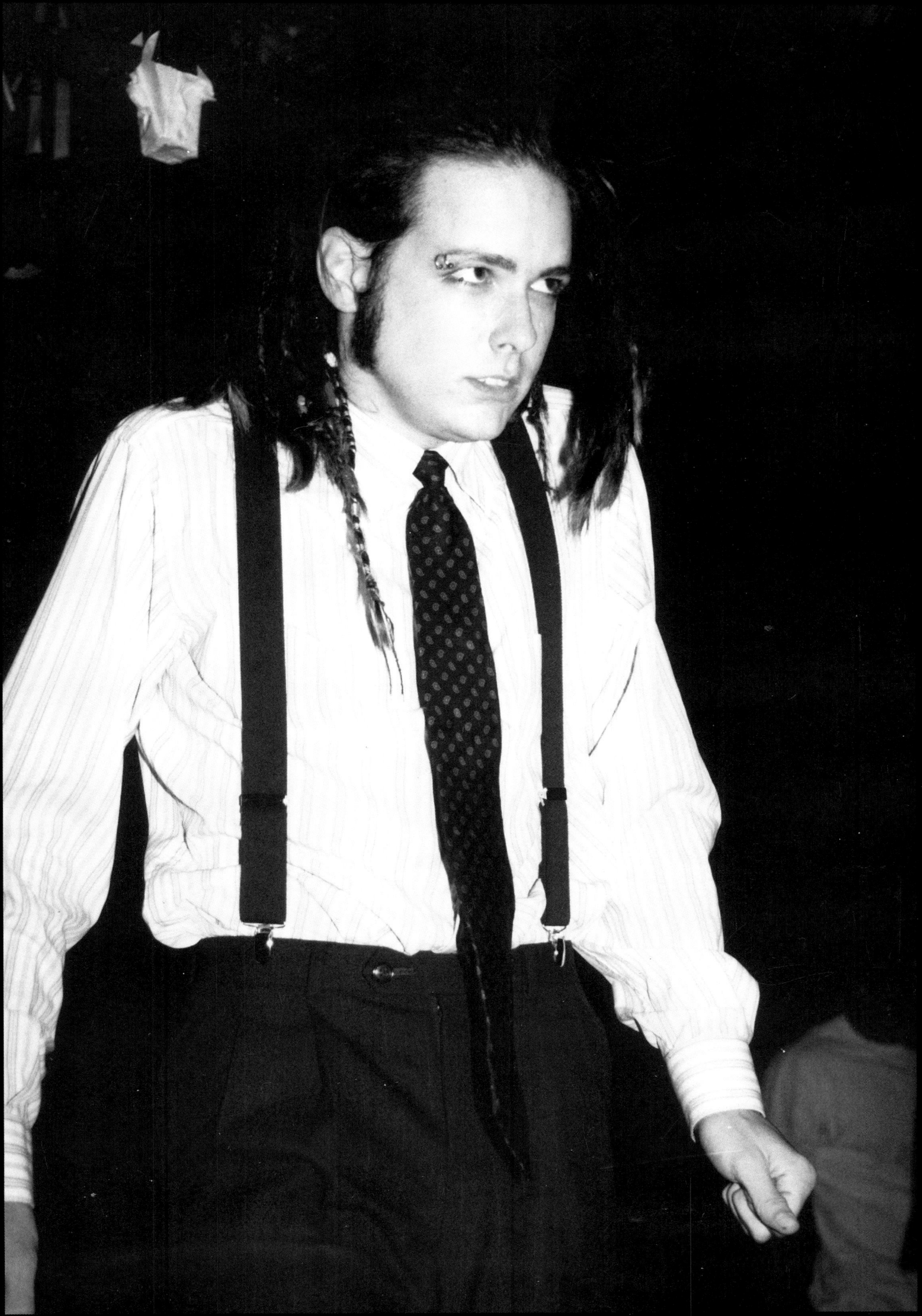

BAGPIPES AND BROOMSTICKS

Korn started the New Year off with a roar, jump-starting a European tour with support acts Urge and Incubus on January 21 at the Markhalle in Hamburg, with another German gig the following night in Bremen. Then it was off to the land of the Scots, to launch an aural assault the likes of which the Glasgow Barrowlands may never before have witnessed. It takes no imagination to conjure up an image of the packed-out venue's reaction when Korn's front man added his legendary bagpipes to the already frenetic stage-show. Climaxing with an unrelenting rendition of "Faget," the show was a pounding, powerful success, and one the band and the crowd will remember as cementing Korn's place in the U.K. music scene. The tour roared on, introducing its ultra-tight and ultra-intense stage show to fans in England's Manchester, Wolverhampton, Nottingham, Leeds, Newcastle, and Bristol. Korn marched onward to whip crowds into a furious frenzy in Amsterdam, Copenhagen, Stockholm, Oslo, Berlin, Munich, Vienna, Milan, Marseilles, Toulouse, Madrid, Barcelona, Strasbourg, and Paris before returning to Germany. They triumphantly wrapped up the month of February with a rescheduled February 24 appearance at London's Brixton Academy, where the band broke the legendary venue's records as the entire floor, from the stage to the bars at the very back, transformed into one giant mosh-pit before the band had finished their opening song.

Korn treats its support bands like one of their own, ensuring that they get equal rights and treatment, in some instances even chipping in out of the collective Korn pocket to foot catering bills. Claiming that every band they ever played support for treated them as substantially less than royalty with the sole exception of Metallica, Korn knows exactly what it's like, and they haven't forgotten. Korn took headlining the bill as a responsibility, not a license to act holier than thou.

In their usual nonstop style, the band barely took time to have their passports stamped and do a bit of laundry before hitting the stage again as they set forth on a whirlwind North American tour, filling halls, ballrooms, auditoriums, and arenas in Arizona, Colorado, Kansas, Louisiana, Florida, Georgia, Kentucky, Ohio, Wisconsin, Minnesota, and Illinois before swinging up to terrorize a few Canadian fans in Toronto. The tour, with hardcore outfit Helmet as opening act, rounded off the month of March with barely a day off with a gig in Maine. In April of 1997 David Silveria married his girlfriend Shannon Bellino, and had her name tattooed on his back. The couple had a baby boy, David, Jr., on August 22.

The bigwigs were beginning to take note. *Rolling Stone*'s Eric Gladstone conceded in April 1997, "Korn are a shining example that performing remains a viable path to success and a reminder that even major-label bands need grassroots support." The notion that perhaps the constant touring and resulting word-of-mouth wildfire-like spread of popularity was not a mapped-out plan of attack with the sole goal of success with a capital S doesn't seem to occur. As we know, Korn did try to get a bit of radio, major music media, and MTV support right at the start. They soon realized, however, that that just wasn't happening, and so decided, in typical Korn style, to "fuck all that" and just get on with it.

In April the band donated a Korned-up Adidas track suit to the T.J. Martell Foundation internet charity auction. Korn is connected with various charities, and this time helped raise money for AIDS, leukemia, and cancer research, and also linked the name of Korn for the first and surely the last time to the likes of co-donators Pamela Anderson, Jerry Seinfeld, and the cast of *Friends*.

The summer of Korn blasted on, with the band touring in Australia and Europe, from the ultra-heavy metal Dynamo festival to the oh-so-trendy Brit-pop Essential festival. Korn broadcast over the web a live cybercast of their London Brixton Academy gig. All of this was mere warmup for the then-confirmed stint with the summer of 1997's most eagerly anticipated musical event: Lollapalooza. While 1996's Lollapalooza wasn't

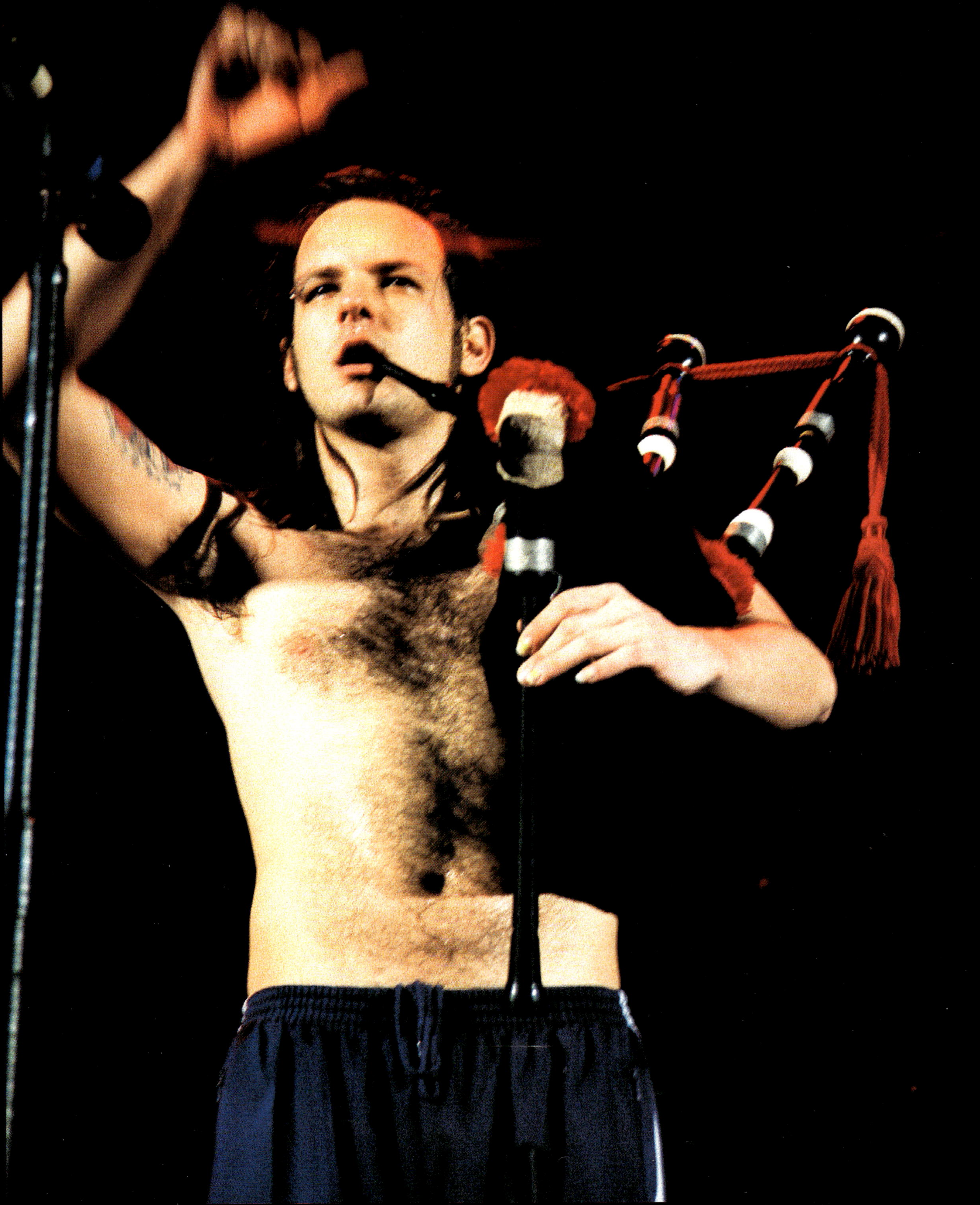

labeled "heavy metal," it was decidedly metal-heavy, as evidenced by festival founder Perry Farrell's absence. Farrell, an indie pioneer and champion, was none too thrilled with the previous year's Metallica-headed line-up of his supposedly diverse and experimental brainchild, but gave the '97 festival his stamp of approval; his band, Porno for Pyros, hit the stage for the opening Lolla date in Florida's West Palm Beach. Korn were set to be the heaviest act on the bill, playing alongside the likes of electronic acts Orbital and the Orb, the witchcraft of Tricky, the mayhem of Prodigy, Tool, UK act James, seminal electronic pioneers Devo, and Snoop Doggy Dogg, who described the scene to MTV News by saying, "It's just music, and we just people, and that's all it's about and that's what this tour represents." Munky put in his vote of approval by saying, "I think that's what Perry's original idea was—to bring a lot of different styles of music together ... just so everybody would have a good time and appreciate the different styles of music and open their minds to some different stuff." When asked by MTV's Serena Altschul whether the band felt threatened by fans who came to the festival to see other bands, whether Korn was worried that their own music wouldn't make the grade when faced with an unfamiliar audience, Fieldy's response was, "It makes us push harder and want to win the crowd over. It doesn't matter. We'll go out if nobody's heard us of and we'll just, we'll push harder and make 'em like us." And if anyone's capable of pushing harder, it's got to be Korn.

Korn played their asses off, barbecued backstage with their new friend Snoop Doggy Dogg, and were mobbed by over 1,000 fans when they attempted to have a chat with a few kids offstage. But not even a month into Lollapalooza, Korn played its last Lolla gig on July 18 due to Munky's ill health. He was diagnosed with a very serious and possibly life-threatening disease, viral meningitis, and hospitalized. Jonathan Davis issued a written statement saying, "We love our fans. This is the last thing we want to do, but it's the only decision to make at this time. It just doesn't feel right without Munky." The band's statement declared that "there is no suitable replacement for Munky during his recuperation."

Korn is most definitely of the all for one, one for all school of thought. Each band member agrees that as their songs come together in the studio, the elements that each man in Korn contribute serve only to further enhance and improve the music. They are quick to praise one another's talents, and seem genuinely impressed and thrilled with the tricks up each other's sleeves. Their tight, never-disappointing live shows are not simply the result of years of practice; here is a band that well and truly clicks, and to substitute another musician just to fill a commitment would never occur to them. Their collective songwriting process, and the insistence that all profit from their music's publishing is split evenly for each and every tune, further testifies to the tight-knit nature of this musical family. Not for Korn the jealousy, competition, and ego-rides that are so typical in the world of rock 'n' roll. They've happened, luckily, upon a better method to the madness of it all, and the result can be heard loud and clear. The band's solidarity paid off: a fully recovered Munky joined his fellow band members in the studio before the summer was out to start brainstorming, jamming, and laying down tracks for what was to become the blockbuster album *Follow the Leader*.

As the end of the long, hard road out of hell that was three years of constant touring, the band members were well and truly knackered: sick and tired. Munky revealed to *Alternative Press* for its September 1997 issue that "coming off stage after some shows, I'd just lock myself in the bathroom and cry my head off because I was so spent, so exhausted. I had to start reminding myself while I was onstage to save like ten percent for myself, for later." Fieldy has described the intensity of the onstage show as being almost impossible to handle, admitting to being physically sick beforehand, afterward, and, on occasion, during the show. Jonathan professes to need a twenty-minute cool-down session immediately after coming offstage. He tried to put into words what happens onstage, saying to *Metal Hammer* in February 1997, "It's like doing a drug. When we're up on stage, it's like going to that place where you're not even aware of it and once the show's over, it's gone, you don't even remember." "When I'm up there I feel, like, sick," Munky revealed in the *Who Then Now?* video. "Really what it is, is the person I don't like in me, all the things I hate in myself—that's who I am up there." Looking back, they know that the grueling, draining three years of spreading the Korn word were necessary, and worth it, but fucking hard work.

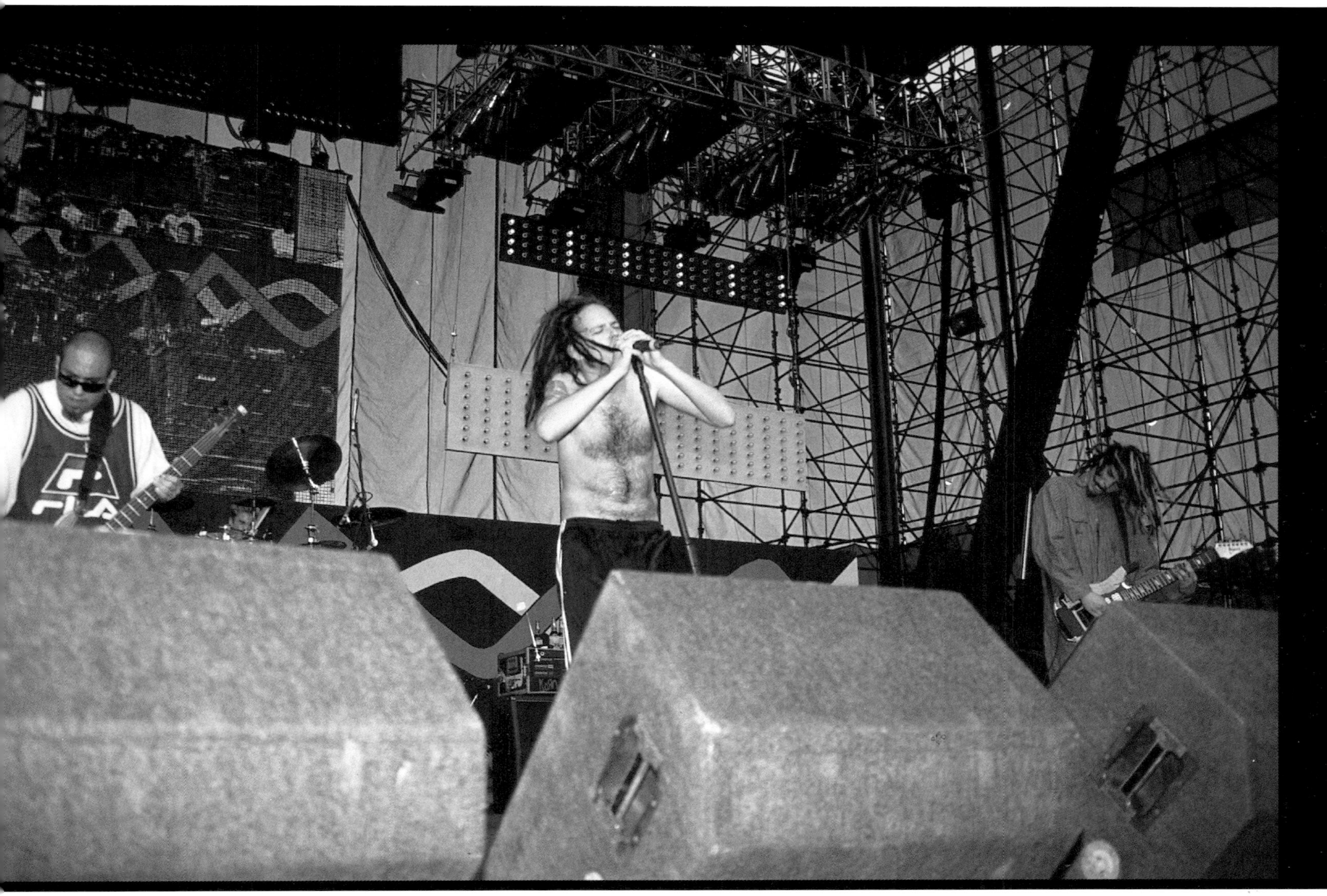

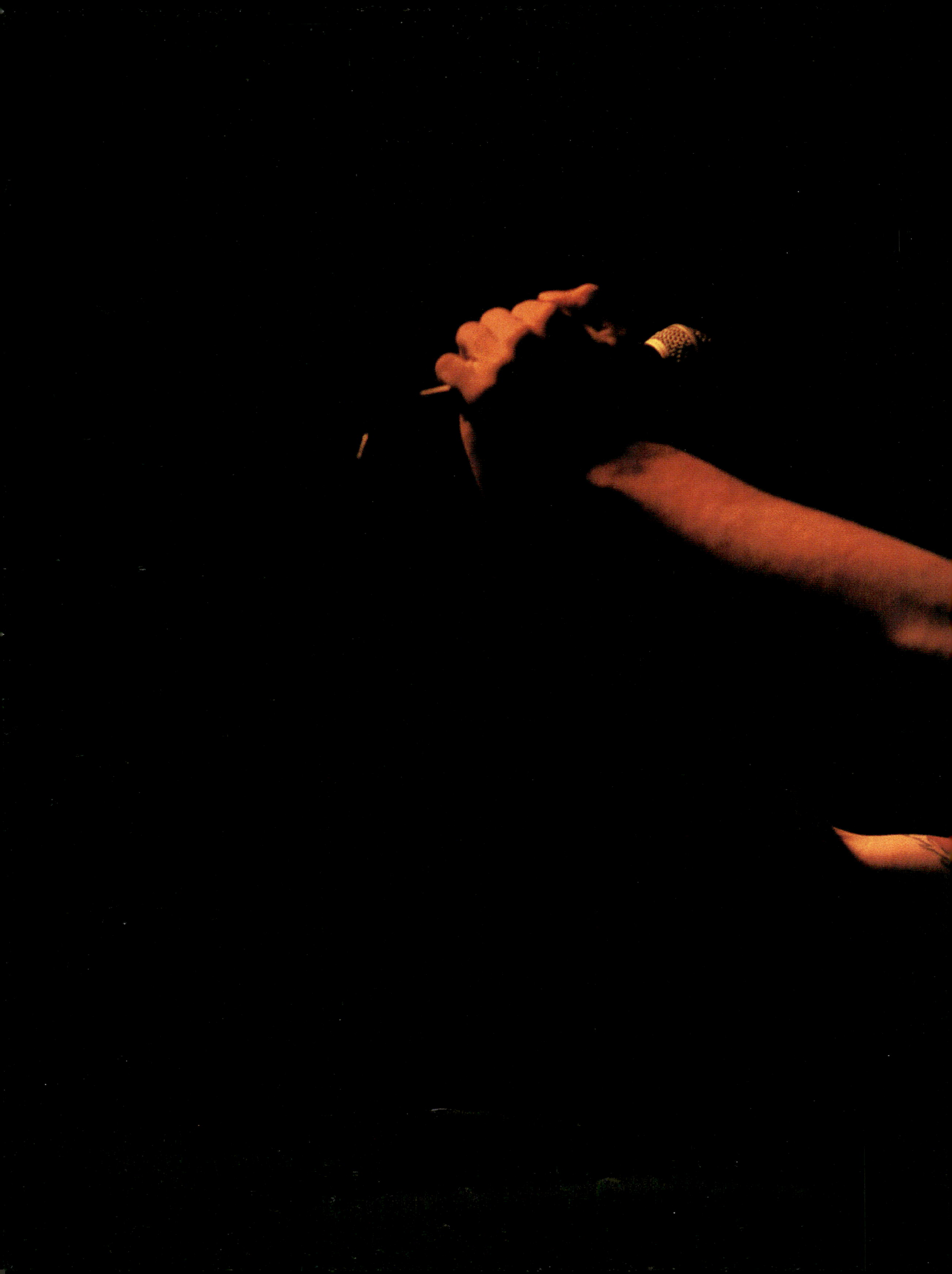

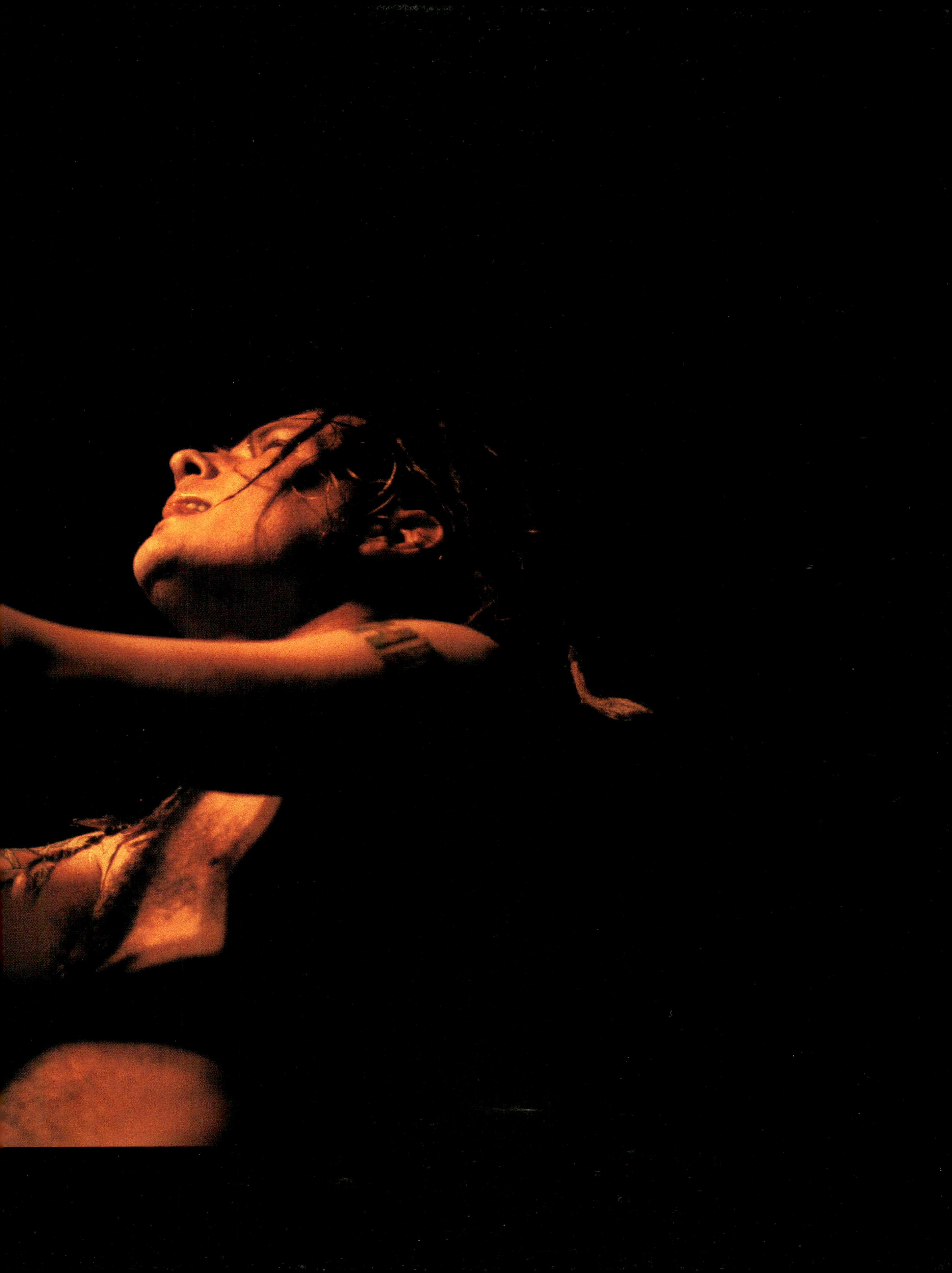

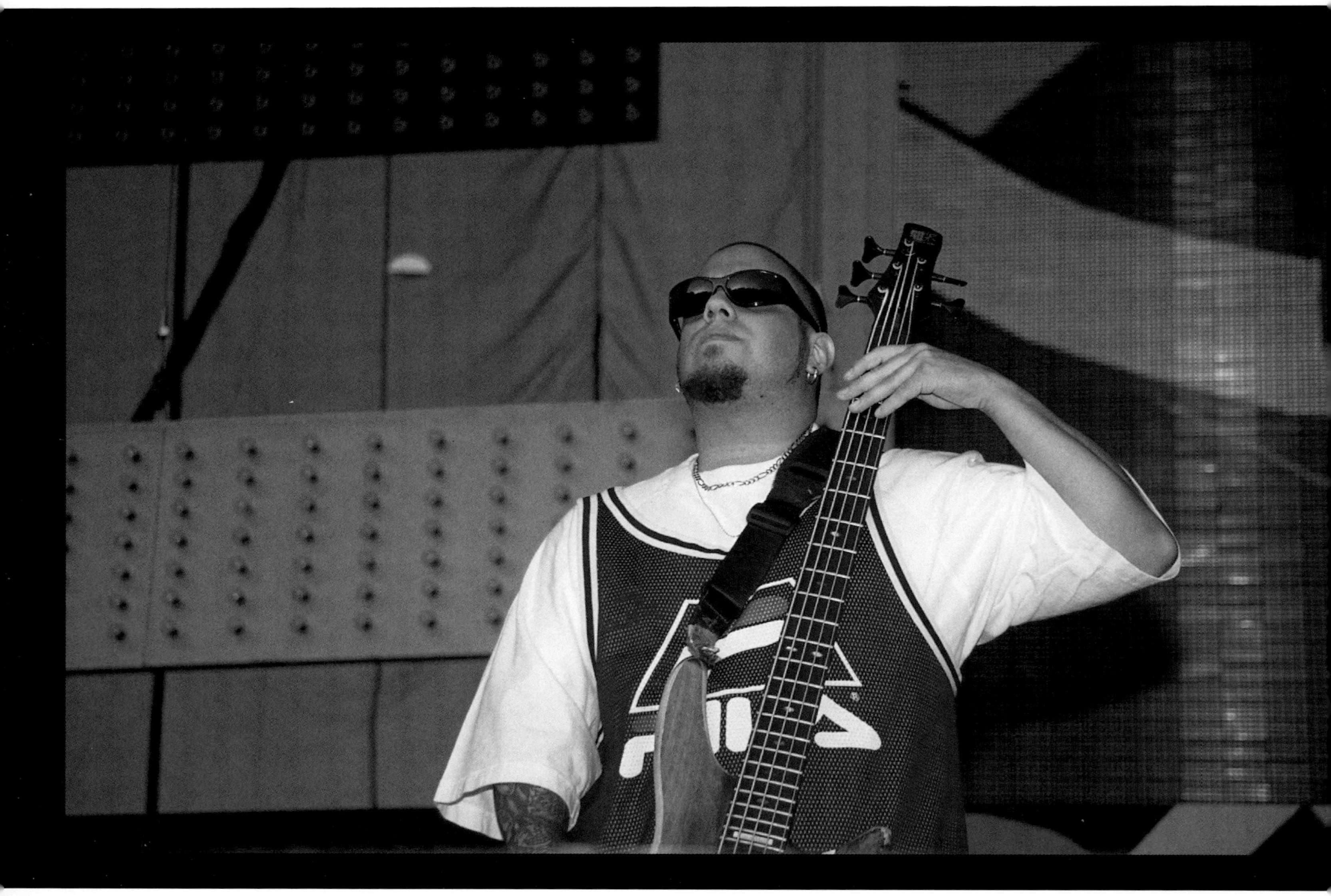

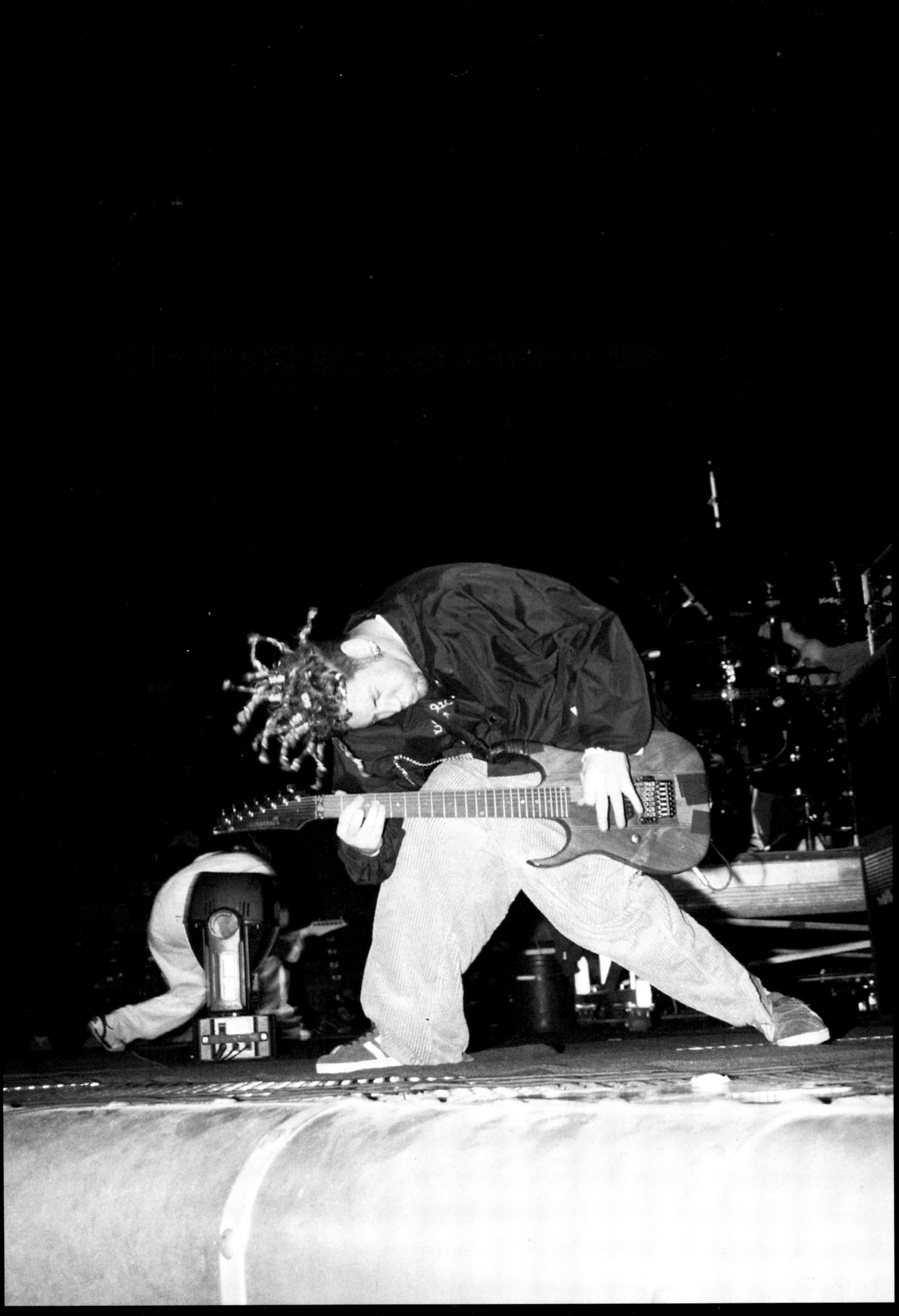

IT'S ON!

Time now to relax? Sit back and take it easy? Not quite. Not content to simply create an all-new album, Korn had a few more tricks up its collective sleeve. The band celebrated Thanksgiving by announcing that they were launching their very own record label. Elementree Records, distributed by Reprise Records, with the very qualified executive team of Jonathan Davis, Brian Welch, James Shaffer, Reginald Arvizu, and David Silveria at the helm, signed its first band, the glam-punk Californian outfit known as Orgy, whose self-described sound is "death pop." Record "exec" Davis says of his new fledgling band, "It's something fresh and new—that's what turns me on. I think they'll appeal to a lot of kids, a lot of different people. They're fashionable pretty-dudes, so all the chicks will dig 'em. And they're real heavy, so hopefully a lot of our friends will like them, too." Orgy, an outfit made up of singer Jay Gordon; Ryan Schuck from the old SexArt days on guitar; Amir Derakh, "guitar synth wizard;" and Paige Haley, bassist; would release their debut album, *Candyass*, on the very same day that Korn's third album hit the charts. Schuck described *Candyass* as "a raw record. It's all five-in-the-morning, pissed-off, fighting-with-each-other, kill-each-other kinda stuff. There's an innovative, futuristic feel to the music." Lead singer Gordon calls the band's music "pretty much just all bullshit ... a bunch of lies and fairy tales." Elementree Records second signing was none other than Cradle of Thorns.

Another Kool-as-Korn announcement served to break in the New Year: the Family Values Tour. In conjunction with the band's management company The Firm's partners Jeff Kwatinetz and Michael Green and Metropolitan Entertainment Group's John Scher, Korn made official their plans to take their own show on the road. Set to hit the road in September, after the jam-packed roster of sweaty summer festivals had wound down, this was going to be different, Korn style. Not the usual outdoor amalgam of sounds, smells, and styles, this was to be a stadium-only, evening-only, rocking show. The kind your grandfather told you about. As Fieldy, in his usual no-bullshit way, told *Metal Edge* magazine, "We hate playing outdoors 'cause the sound sucks. When you see a rock 'n' roll band you want to see them in the dark, with lights, everything. I don't think there's any vibe at all at an outdoor show. It looks like four dudes standing there with guitars." To keep things moving and cut down on, well, down-time in between acts, they invested in a revolving stage. The tour was set to include Orgy, White Zombie's Rob Zombie gone solo, German industrial metal group Rammstein, Ice Cube, Limp Bizkit, and, of course, Korn. The Deftones, despite their close friendship with Korn members, declined to join the Family Values tour allegedly due to a bit of an ego problem, as they didn't fancy being one step down on the bill ladder from Limp Bizkit. Jonathan told *Billboard* in its September 26, 1998, issue that Korn were friends with all of the bands on the tour with the exception of Rammstein, whom they had yet to meet; he seemed confident that the bands would gel, however, saying, "But they blow themselves up, and they're German, so getting along should be easy. We plan to party a lot."

Well, what with planning your own no-holds-barred summer festival, recording a new album, and orchestrating your own new label, you find yourself with a lot of time on your hands. In March the Korn collective went one step cooler, and blasted their own internet TV show over the cyberspace airwaves at www.kornTV.com. KornTV, a weekly, hour-long live audio and video transmission from Korn's studio, was a truly unprecedented concept. What better way to make their fans feel like they really are part of the action than inviting them to spend an hour with the band once a week?

The live antics of the Korn guys proved to be just as outrageous and fun as their eager fans expected. The show featured live calls from fans (including "some goyl in Joisey"); lots of bizarre guest stars, like Fred "Re-Run" Berry of conventional TV's 70s show *What's Happening*; fellow musicians galore with members of 311, Orgy, Sugar Ray, Pharcyde, the Deftones, Limp Bizkit; as well as Bobbie Brown, Loveline's Adam Carolla, and Steve Vai showing up. Guitar virtuoso Vai proclaimed his admiration for Korn's unique sound, saying in *Guitar World*'s June 1998 issue, "It's quite a sonic overload. One day I was

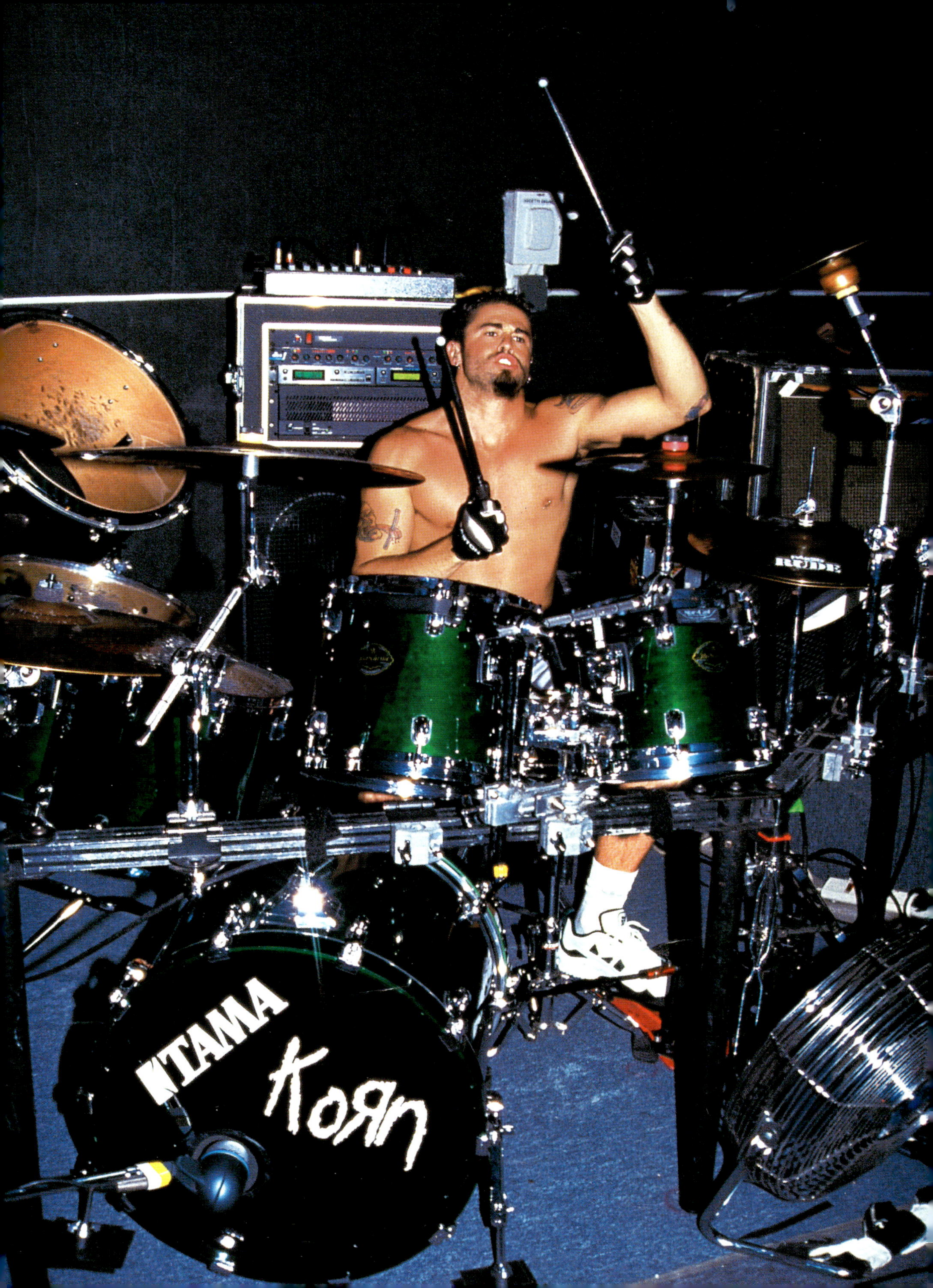
TAMA
KoRn
RUDE

coming from the zoo and heard Korn on the radio. I was stunned. It sounded like a herd of buffalo wearing iron shoes and blowing fire out of their nostrils." The guest list was quite a mixture. Add to this the sometimes drunken antics and spontaneous performances of Korn themselves, Munky and Jonathan's hairstyling advice for dreadlocked fans, and a bit of kinky stuff professional-style and you've got a hell of a show on your hands. The kinkyness was courtesy of Dominic the Rope Artist, who made an appearance on the truly unforgettable April 2 episode of the *After School Specials*. Dominic obligingly whipped and tied porn star Randy Rage while Munky and Jonathan (completely innocent bystanders) looked on, and topped it all off with a bit of electrical stimulation. Fetish is as fetish does. Sure brightens up a day spent at boring old school, though. Of course, this type of thing has been a hobby of sorts for the Korn singer for some time; Jonathan's January 18 birthday party at the Union featured strippers and a bondage show.

The Korn website describes the KornTV recording studio set as "a middle-Eastern vibe with multicolored carpets lining the floor and ceilings, dim lights, candles, and incense—plus the band's infamous collection of porno on the walls, and of course, the immense supply of 'ice coldies' (that's beer in Korn slang)." The show wrapped up its season on April 16 with the promise of an August grand finale and went into rerun mode. But not to worry: Korn fans craving something new could visit The Palace, "the world's premiere graphical chat system," which allowed netsurfers worldwide to visit the virtual world of Korn Korner.

March proved to be a month not only for After School Specials, but for In School Controversy. An innocent little Korn T-shirt caused a major First Amendment issue at a small Michigan high school. Zeeland High School student Eric VanHoven was actually suspended from school for the grave offense of wearing a T-shirt with the word "Korn" on it. The rules of the school forbade the wearing of "any clothing or items that imply obscenity, violence, drugs, alcohol, or sexual innuendo." Needless to say, this ruling reeked a bit of a violation of some fairly basic rights to fellow students and a large segment of the local population. The shit, as they say, hit the fan. Petitions against such violation of civil liberties were signed by parents and students alike. VanHoven's best friend, Matt Maldonado, was also suspended and told the *Holland Sentinel* that "hicks, preps, rappers, people from all different cliques are signing this (petition) because they're afraid the school will ban something else next." Television crews turned up to film a Grand Rapids radio station, WKLQ, giving away hundreds of free Korn T-shirts outside the school one afternoon as the students emerged from classes. It was a mob scene, and the Ottawa County Sheriff's police department helped the station hand out the shirts (kindly donated by the band) while the chanting of anticensorship slogans filled the air. MTV News interviewed the eighteen-year-old VanHoven. Gretchen Plewes, the vice-principal, explained her rationale behind suspending VanHoven in the *Holland Sentinel* by citing the

(fifty)

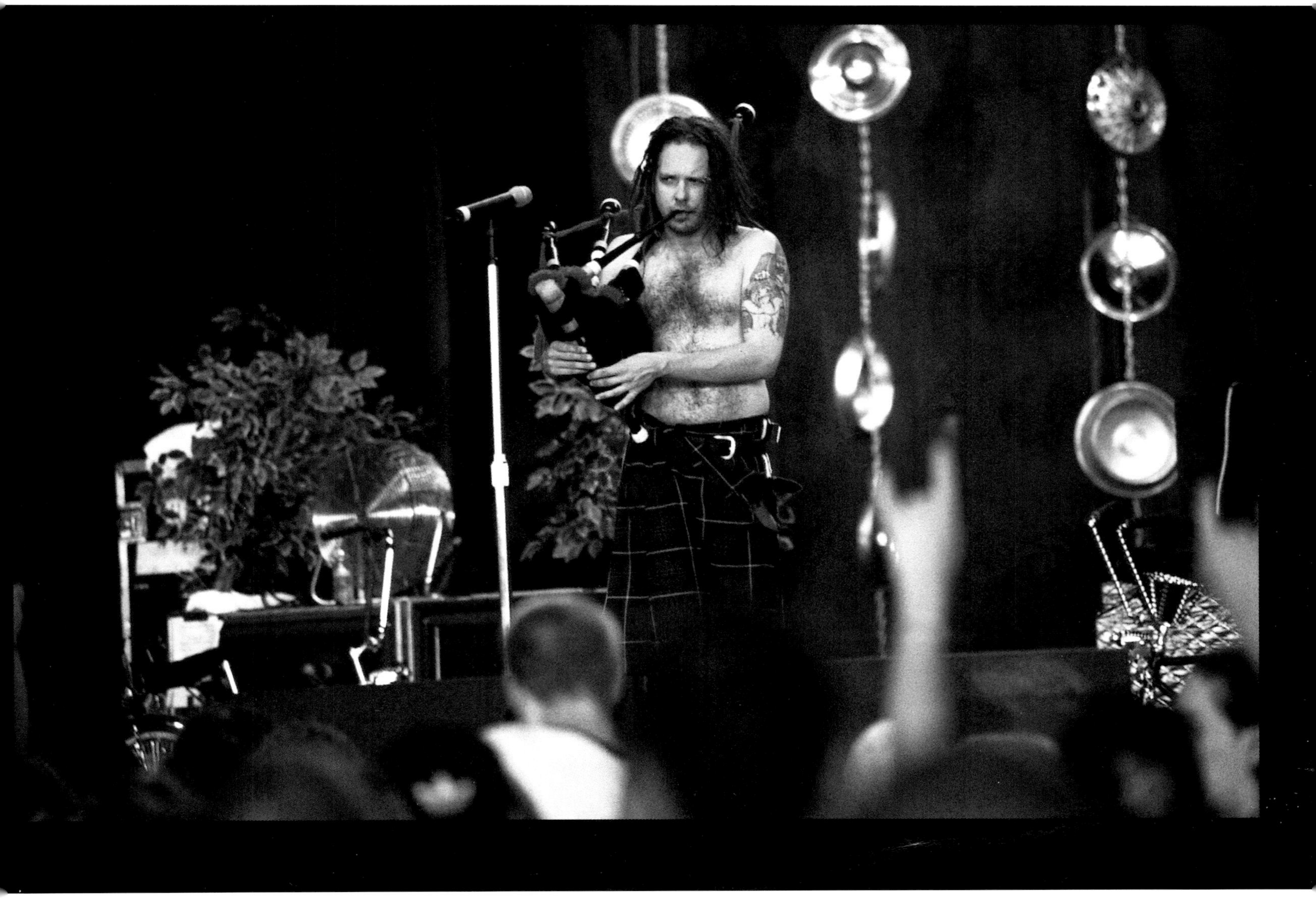

band's "extremely offensive lyrics." She went on to the make the statement that "Korn is indecent, vulgar, obscene, and intends to be insulting. It is no different than a person wearing a middle finger on their shirt." JAM TV interviewed Zeeland Public School District Spokesman Jim Camenga who revealed that "the Korn lyrics we've seen on the Internet do not reflect our community's standards." Presumably the high school students should be counted as part of the community, but this point was apparently lost on the top dog of the school system. VanHoven got himself an attorney, Kary Love, who asked, "If our right to free speech doesn't protect just one word, what does it protect? How many words are left?" She was also quoted as stating, "The scary thing is that any clothing could imply obscenity under the school's classification. Kids wear shirts that say 'Jesus Saves.' That implies the Bible, which is filled with 3,000 years worth of violence and sex."

Korn did not take T-shirt-gate lightly. The band promptly dispatched a cease-and-desist order against Plewes and the school district for their defamatory comments. News that the band was also in consultation with its attorneys about plans to file a multimillion dollar lawsuit abounded, with Korn reportedly resolving to forward all proceeds to charities fighting child abuse and the American Civil Liberties Union. In an official statement issued by the band, Fieldy said, "Lack of radio, major press, and MTV airplay couldn't stop Korn, so what makes some small-town assistant principal think that she can?" Jonathan went on the air with WKLQ, saying, "It's been a really shocking experience for us to hear something as ridiculous.... We'll stick up for our fans. They should be able to wear our shirts wherever they want." Korn's management was equally up in arms, and Jeff Kwatinetz told JAM TV, "It's stupid for a vice principal to spend her time trying to silence kids who support a band that does charity work and speaks out against child abuse. This is a good illustration of the failure of our educational system."

The Great T-shirt Debate couldn't go on forever, and Korn had work to do. And personal lives to attend to. Fieldy married his girlfriend Shela; their daughter Sarina Rae, born September 30, 1997, will have a new brother or sister soon, as the newlyweds are expecting their second child in December. The band decided against playing their slated gig at the June 20, 1998, Ozzfest UK at the Milton Keynes Bowl, as Head's wife Rebekah was due any moment with the couple's child. The baby, as babies are wont to do, refused to cooperate, and Head's daughter Jennea Marie Welch was born some three weeks late via induced labor on July 6.

Controversy makes the heart grow fonder, or something like that, and Rob Zombie dropping out of the Family Values line-up at the end of July caused a bit of a family feud. The Korn camp press release claimed that Zombie was not keen on Ice Cube's appearance on the bill and "repeatedly lectured that rock kids don't like hip-hop." The White Zombie man claimed in turn that he simply felt he couldn't logistically put on the show he wanted to in support of his new solo album *Hellbilly Deluxe* on such a tour. "You can't build a huge den of Satan and tear it down in five minutes. It's just not possible," he told MTV News. He then put together his own solo tour with Fear Factory and Monster Magnet as support. Limp Bizkit front man Fred Durst gave the tour his wholehearted support in July, telling MTV News, "It's just the right time in music. It's the right time in 1998. It's the best way to end off the year with a big boom. It's gonna be out of control. It's like, the world is so emotional these days, and that's a very emotional bill." Ending the year with a boom was a promise Korn was sure to keep, but before Family Values hit the road on September 22, Korn had some goods to deliver.

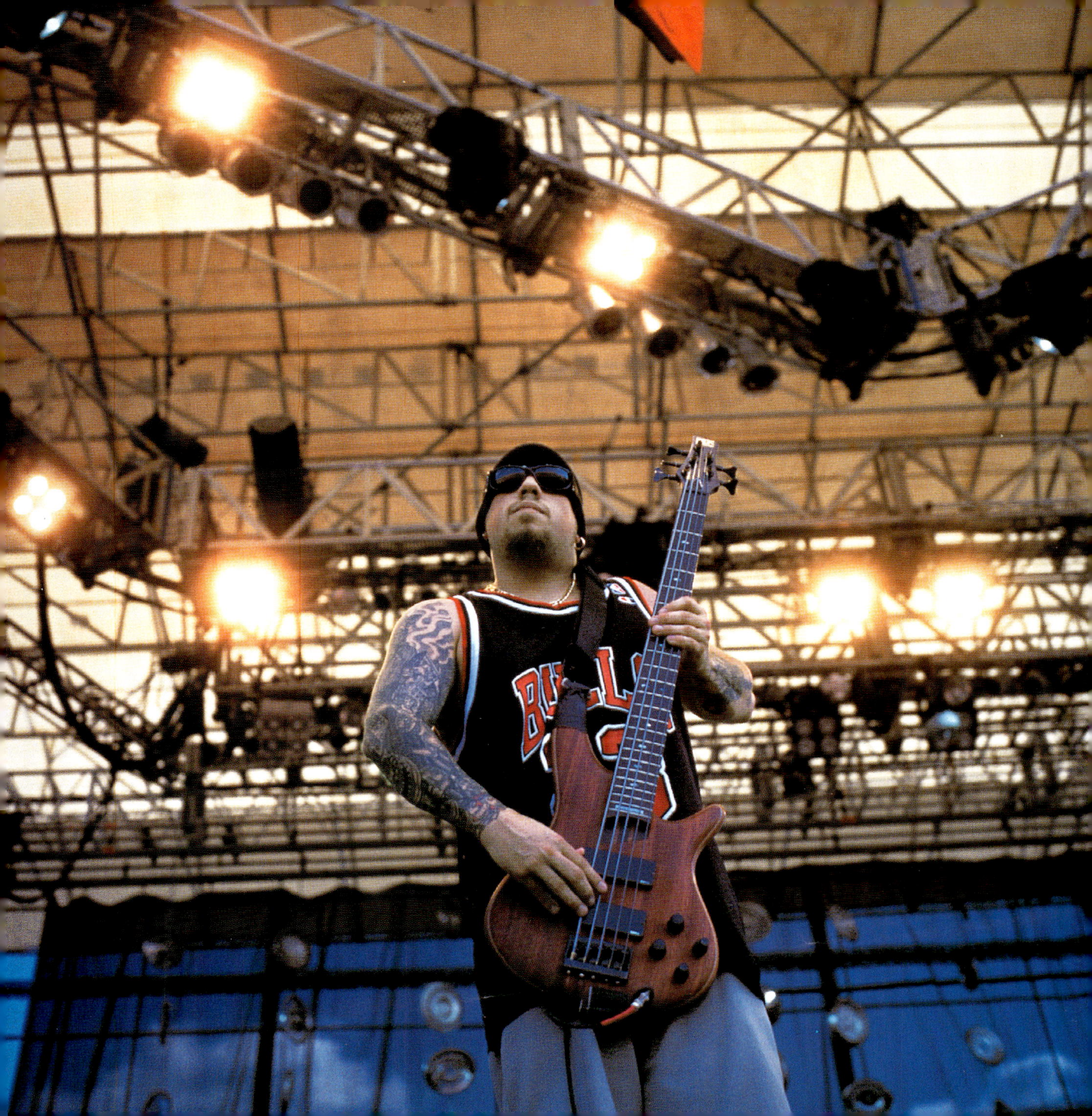

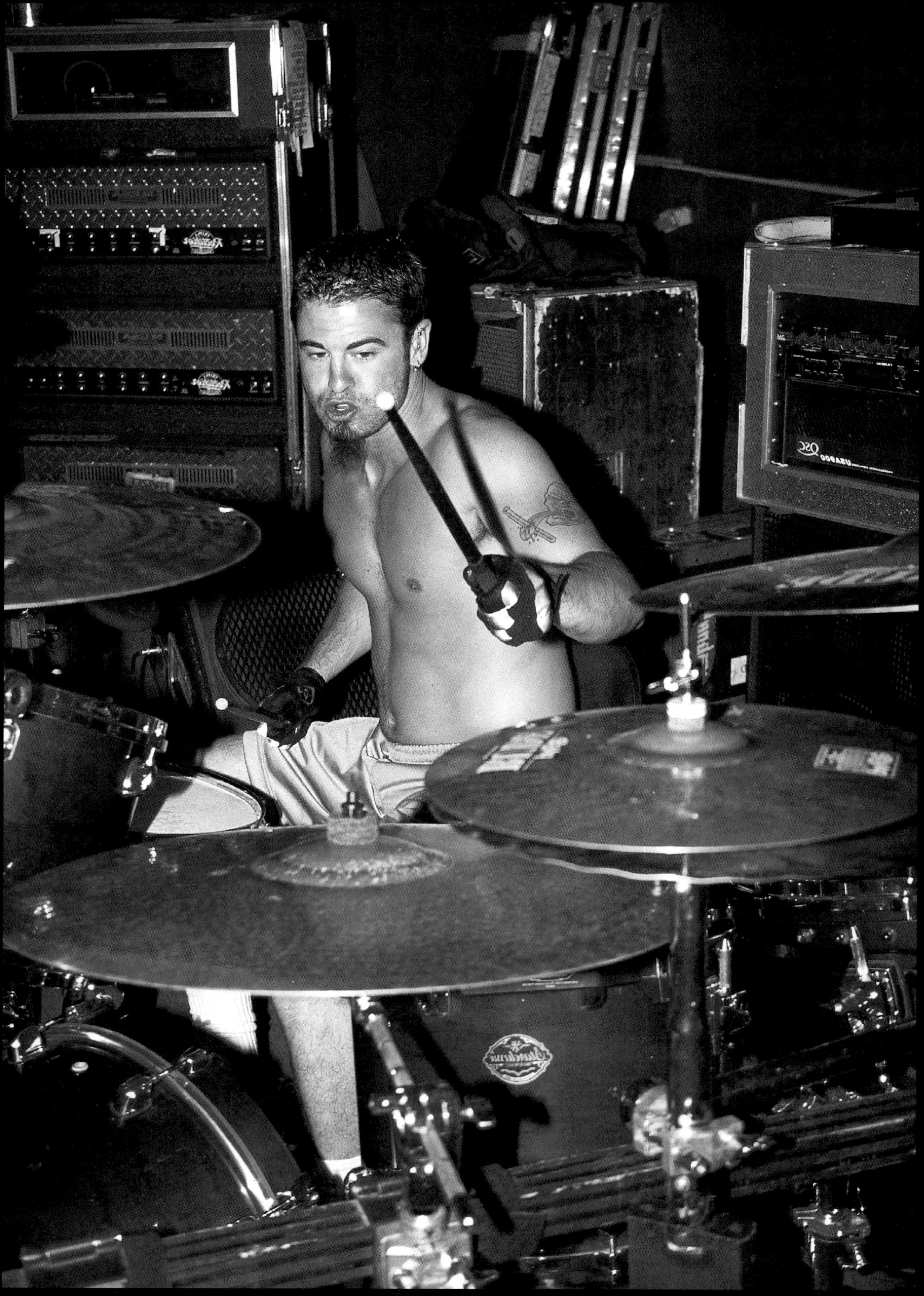

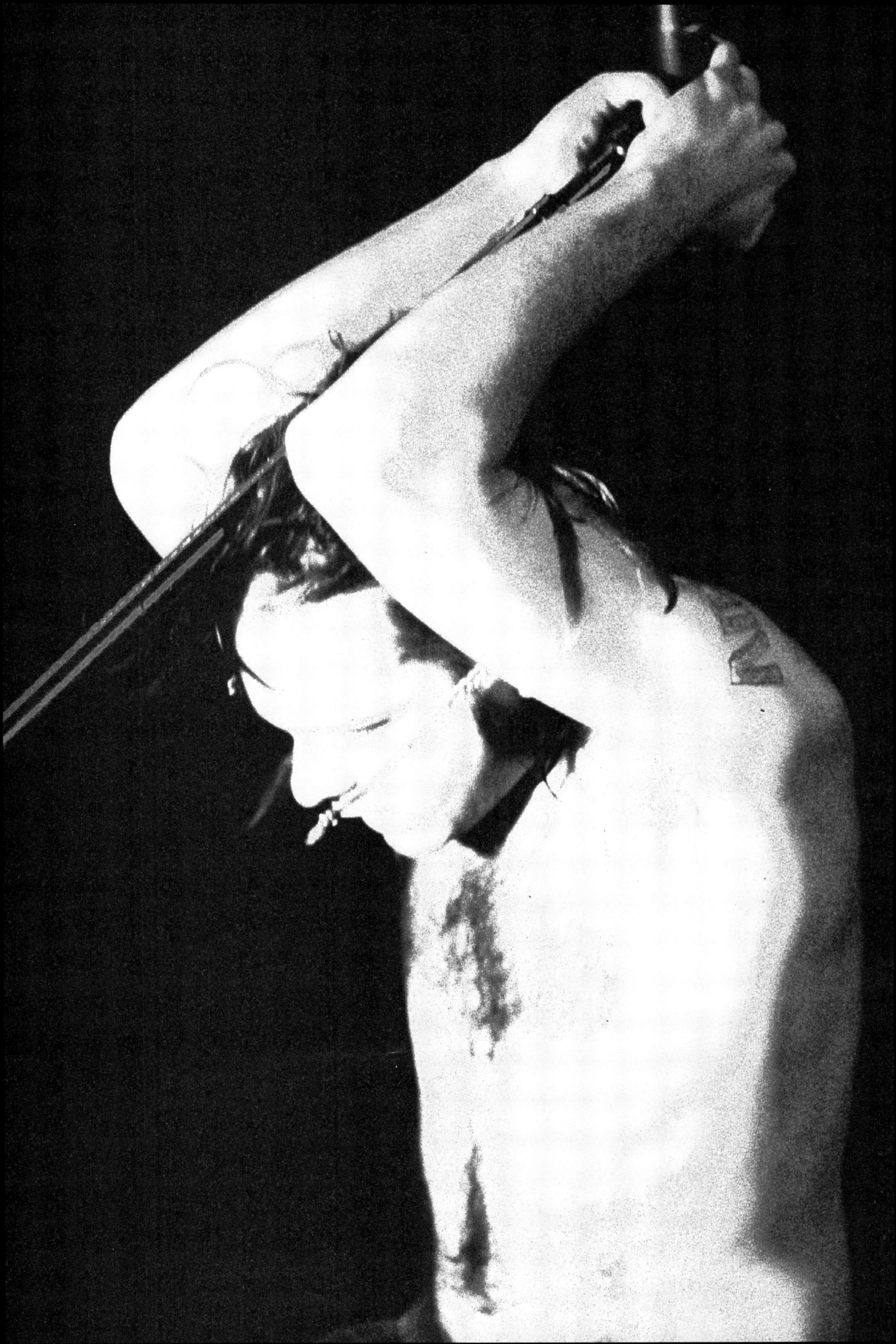

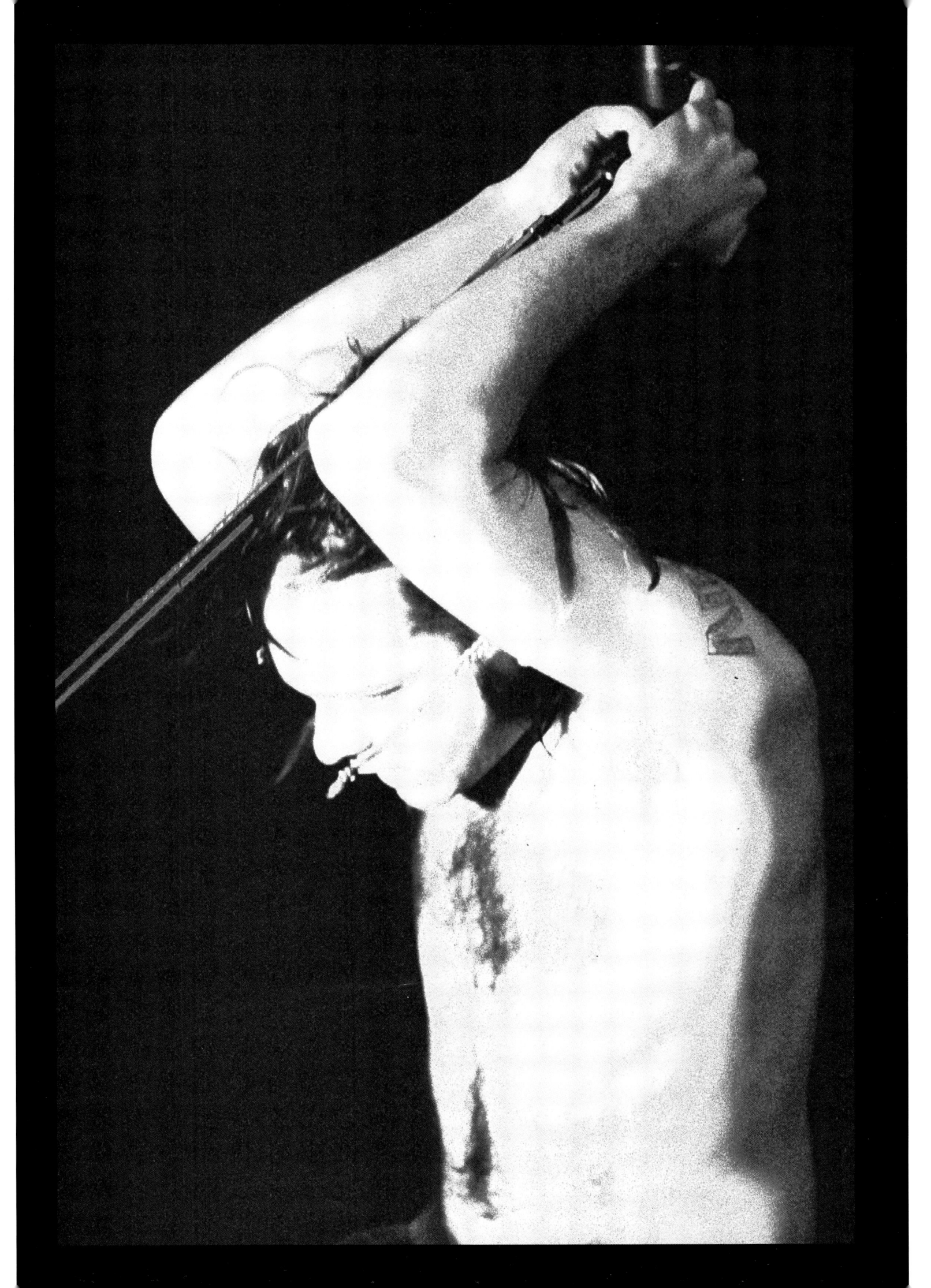

SLASH AND BURN

With *Follow the Leader*, Korn set out to perfect the seminal sound they began trailblazing back in 1993. The pioneers of the new frontier were going all the way this time. The band's enthusiasm for their third album began well before they reached the studio. Dave Silveria was raving about it to *Alternative Press*'s September 1997 issue, predicting, "We're gonna stay in the studio until we have an album full of material where we can say, 'This is the bomb!' We're gonna stuff it with the phattest grooves, the heaviest shit ever. Fuck it—fuck radio, fuck everything—we're just gonna put out the coolest, heaviest thing we can." As Jonathan told *Hit Parader* in its October 1998 issue, "This one is gonna set the standards ... it's the heaviest thing we've ever done. It's the heaviest thing I've ever heard. That's heavy! When we were putting it all together we really wanted to come up with the best of what we do and then really magnify upon each of those elements." He goes on to say that the album is unique in that, despite its heaviness, it's something people can dance to and listen to over and over. He concedes, "Sometimes really heavy albums begin to wear you out. Just listening to them exhausts you. That won't happen with this one."

Follow the Leader debuted on the *Billboard* album charts at Number One in its September 5, 1998, issue, selling 268,000 copies in its first week. Sadly, the momentous event coincided with Jonathan's grandfather's funeral. The album also went in at Number One in Canada, New Zealand, and Australia; Number Four in Finland; Number Five in the U.K., France, and Norway; Number Eight in Japan; Number Ten in Holland; and Number Twelve in Germany. *Rolling Stone* gave the album four stars, concluding its lead review with the warning, "*Follow the Leader* is going to blow up in your face. Prepare to eat shrapnel—whether you like it or not." And, as per usual, the band did not receive a lukewarm reception from anyone—like it or not, indeed. The very magazine that reported *Follow the Leader*'s top debut was not too happy about it, and the review in *Billboard*'s September 12, 1998, issue, complained, "Despite that impressive sales performance, the album offers little in the way of enduring satisfaction. Peddling industrial rock clichés and angst-ridden, often misogynistic lyrics, Korn comes across as a band without a clear purpose or an original sound." To quote the lyrics of Korn classic "Faget," "Suck my dick and fucking like it!"

The album, with its artwork depicting a little girl hop-scotching off the end of a cliff followed by a gaggle of loyal kiddies courtesy of Todd McFarlane, the comic book king and Spawn mastermind, was at once a challenge and an invitation to the decade's stale music scene. As Jonathan told *Metal Edge* magazine in its November 1998 issue, "The '90s sucked for music, basically. Kids are sick of it; they want to hear something heavy, what rock 'n' roll is supposedly all about. With the alternative bands, there was nothing to grasp onto or hold close ... kids are tired of hearing wimpy shit. They want to hear something that gets their adrenaline pumping. For me, that's what music's about." He went on to add that "in the '70s and '80s New Wave, metal, hair bands were cool, it all coexisted. It was fun and exciting. With the grunge scene everything got fucked. I think history repeats itself and it will be rock 'n' roll again." David expressed similar sentiments to *Alternative Press* in September, saying simply, "The whole 'alternative' thing just turned into a mush of shit."

Follow the Leader features a few choice guest stars, including, strangely enough, Cheech Marin. The hidden track at the end of the CD is a suitably twisted cover version of Cheech & Chong's 1978 hit "Earache My Eye" from the soundtrack to *Up In Smoke*. To further add to the song's chaos, Fieldy took over lead vocals, Jonathan became the drummer, David played the bass, and Munky and Head traded places. Also making special appearances on the album are Ice Cube, Cypress Hill's B-Real, Pharcyde's Tré, and Limp Bizkit's Fred Durst, who trades insults with Jonathan on the it's-all-among-friends free-for-all that is "All in the Family."

Selected *Follow the Leader* CD releases were accompanied, courtesy of good old shrink wrap, with a special single edition of "Good God" featuring two remixes of the *Life Is Peachy* song, the "Heartfloor Remix" by none other than Family Values tourmate

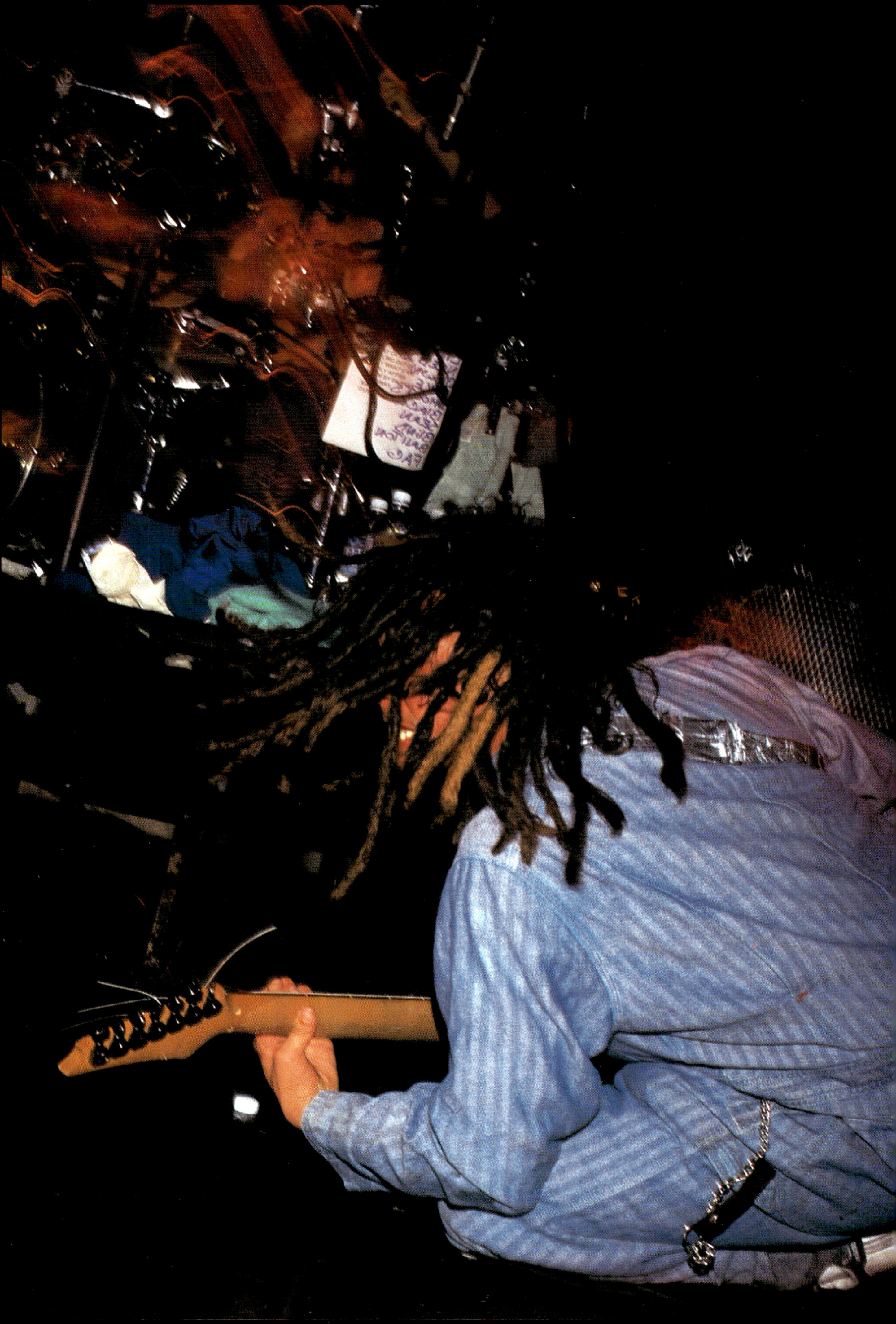

Rammstein, and the "Oomph vs. Such a Surge Remix" by, you guessed it, Such a Surge. Korn also arranged for an Added Values CD, a compilation to feature the likes of Fear Factory, the Propellerheads, and Aphex Twin to be given away with *Follow the Leader*. The first track on the album is track number thirteen, as the band allegedly did not want to end with thirteen, and so decided to begin with it. Tracks one through thirteen are simply five seconds each of silence.

The album was laid down at North Hollywood's NRG Recording. Right in the middle of recording, Korn let producer Steve Thompson (of Guns N' Roses, Butthole Surfers, and Henry Rollins Band fame) go and switched over to Toby Wright, best known for his work with Alice in Chains. Wright was there from the start, working as a part of the *Follow the Leader* team as an engineer. As Jonathan told *Metal Edge* magazine in its November 1998 issue, "Hearing the album now, and the change we made, it was all worth it. When we heard the first mixes it sounded foreign to us, not right, but we were all used to hearing shitty music. Now that I hear it it's 'Oh, my God!' I'm glad we made the change. It was good for us and we deserved it." It's clear that the band is 100% satisfied with the album. "It's Korn Plus," says Head in *Guitar World*'s October 1998 issue. "It's a matured Korn, musically," says Munky. "It still sounds like Korn, but it's more creative. We're really getting in tune with how to play what we're hearing in our heads and how to get the right sounds."

The album's lyrics were reportedly penned during Jonathan's stay at a rather upscale hotel in Hollywood. The hotel's gracious tone did not, needless to say, suit our hero; he was, to put it mildly, not happy with his surroundings. As we have come to know, the words of Korn's music are borne of alienation and rage. So in truth this unnamed lap of luxury was just the spot for a bit of lyricism. As Jonathan put it to *Request* magazine, "All the fucking snobs hang out and the actors, and everyone's so fucking fake there and uptight. I made me so pissed off, and being mad inspires me. Then mix in the alcohol and the walls drop." Being sequestered away in a hotel room, under pressure to write, can tend to bring on an appetite for self-destruction. Oh, did we neglect to mention that Jonathan sought solace in a wee dram of whiskey whilst trying to deal with the crème de la trendy? In fact, the track "B.B.K" is a tribute of sorts to Jonathan's nickname for his poison of choice, Jack Daniels and Coke.

One of many standout tracks, "Justin," was written for a teenage boy with intestinal cancer who, through the Make-a-Wish Foundation, was granted his wish to meet his favorite band. Korn ended up hanging with the boy for days, and Justin watched as the band composed the song. Jonathan was well and truly blown away by the fourteen-year-old's attitude, telling *Alternative Press*, "He knows he's gonna die, but he just has this big smile on his face all the time. And we couldn't even look at the kid at first. It's hard to stare death in the eye. But he just opened it up—he's such a good fuckin' kid—and he started crying when we played his song. We got so attached to this kid, totally forgot he was gonna die."

"My Gift to You" is a song whose basic structure was actually written before Korn was even born; the band decided to take it off the shelf and rework it. Here is the closest Korn's lead singer comes to writing a love ballad. Words don't come easily to describe the twisted nature of this one, but rest assured a Celine Dion version is not on the cards. "Fuckin' sick," is how Jonathan himself described it to *Alternative Press*. "It's my fantasy of fucking my wife and killing her. And she loved it! We have a weird relationship." Tales of Mrs. Davis leaving "love notes" under Mr. Davis's pillow detailing the many ways she'd like to murder her husband have been often cited as evidence of the couple's unconventional take on that thing called love.

Perhaps at once the most moving and most repellent moment on the album comes within the song "Pretty." Here Jonathan sings about preparing the tiny body of a sexually abused baby girl for burial with the words, "I see a pretty face/ Smashed against the bathroom floor/ What a disgrace/ Who do I feel sorry for?"

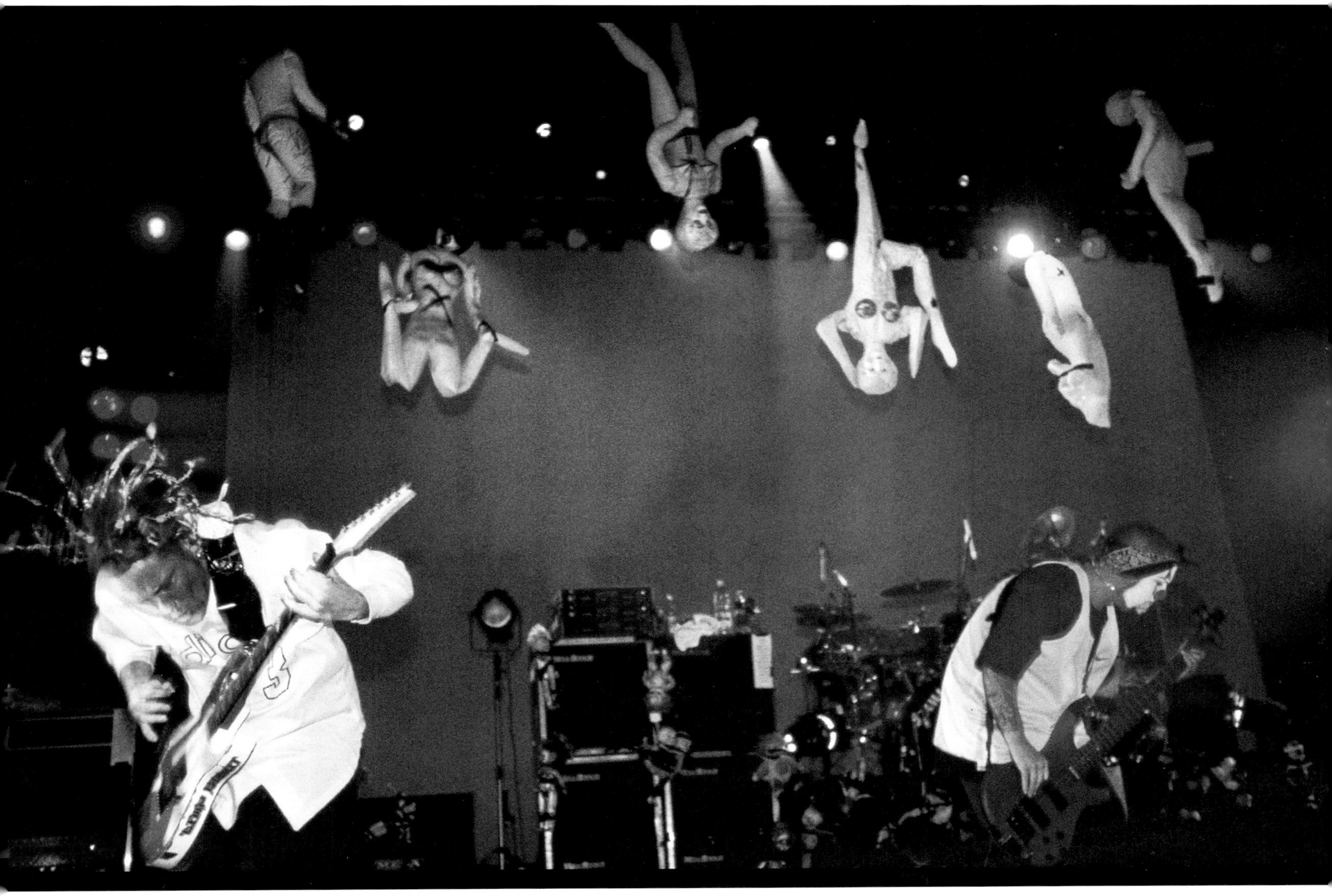

The album's first single, "Got the Life," is a less than four-minute blend of the strongest elements of Korn. Jonathan's vocals run the gamut of demented whines to gut-rumbling growls, and the unholy sounds Munky, Fieldy, and Head manage to pull out of their hats are driven by a beat worthy of any shit-hot disco tune, courtesy of Dave's precision drumming. The song is an argument of sorts between God and Jonathan; God insists to the rock star, "you've already got the life," in response to his discontented pleadings. The video, a definite breakthrough for Korn, is a showcase of fast cars, glamour and glitz, and all the smiling sycophants that come with The Life. We are treated to a different Jonathan here: his darkened hair and non-Adidas velvet coat might be part of the shift, but it seems that the offstage Jonathan Davis can be glimpsed here, holding his head in his hands in the backseat of a limousine.

To well and truly launch *Follow the Leader*, Korn came up with yet another brainstorm: The Korn Kampaign '98. A private-jet-fueled "political" campaign which whizzed the band around North America to meet and greet their fans, sign a few thousand autographs, and maybe even kiss a lucky baby or two, the Kampaign was a roaring success. Too much of a success, as a matter of fact. The "kornference" stop in New York City's Greenwich Village ended up in pandemonium. As reported on korn.com, a police sergeant at the scene (one of 200 dispatched to babysit the 7,000 strong crowd) declared, "This was the biggest in-store we've ever seen in New York City, and even crazier than when the Spice Girls were here." And that, apparently, is saying something.

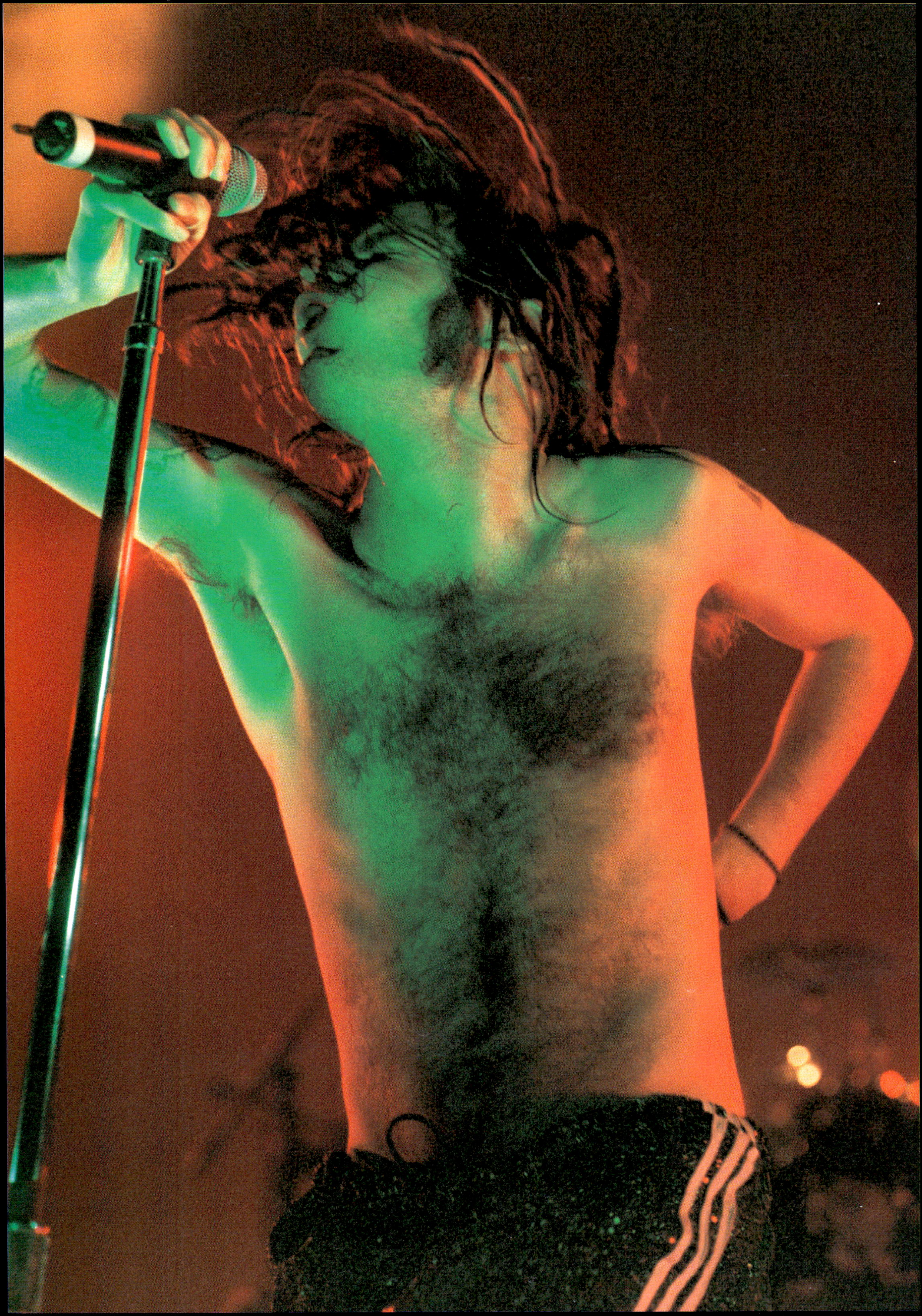

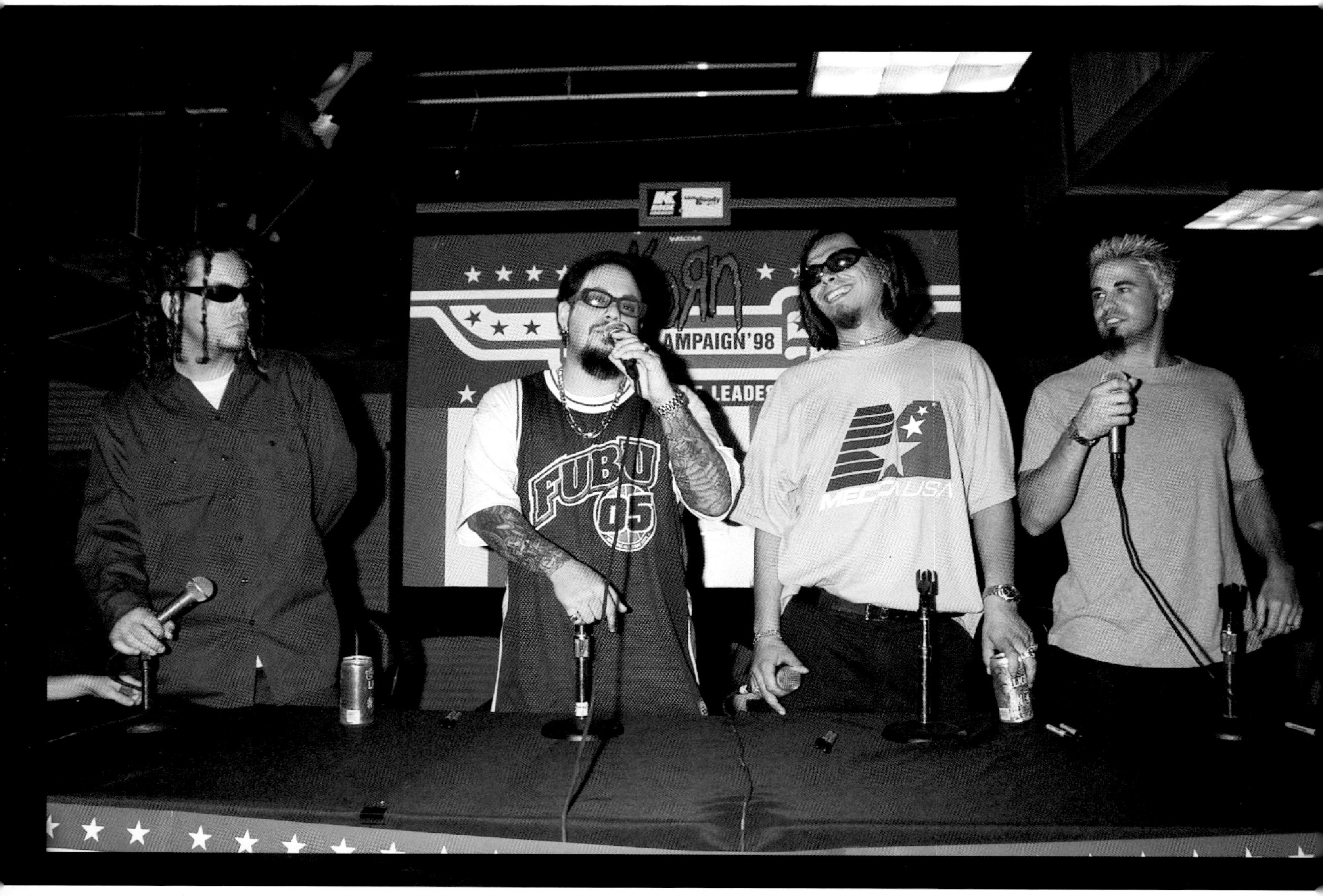
AMPAIGN'98
FUBU
05

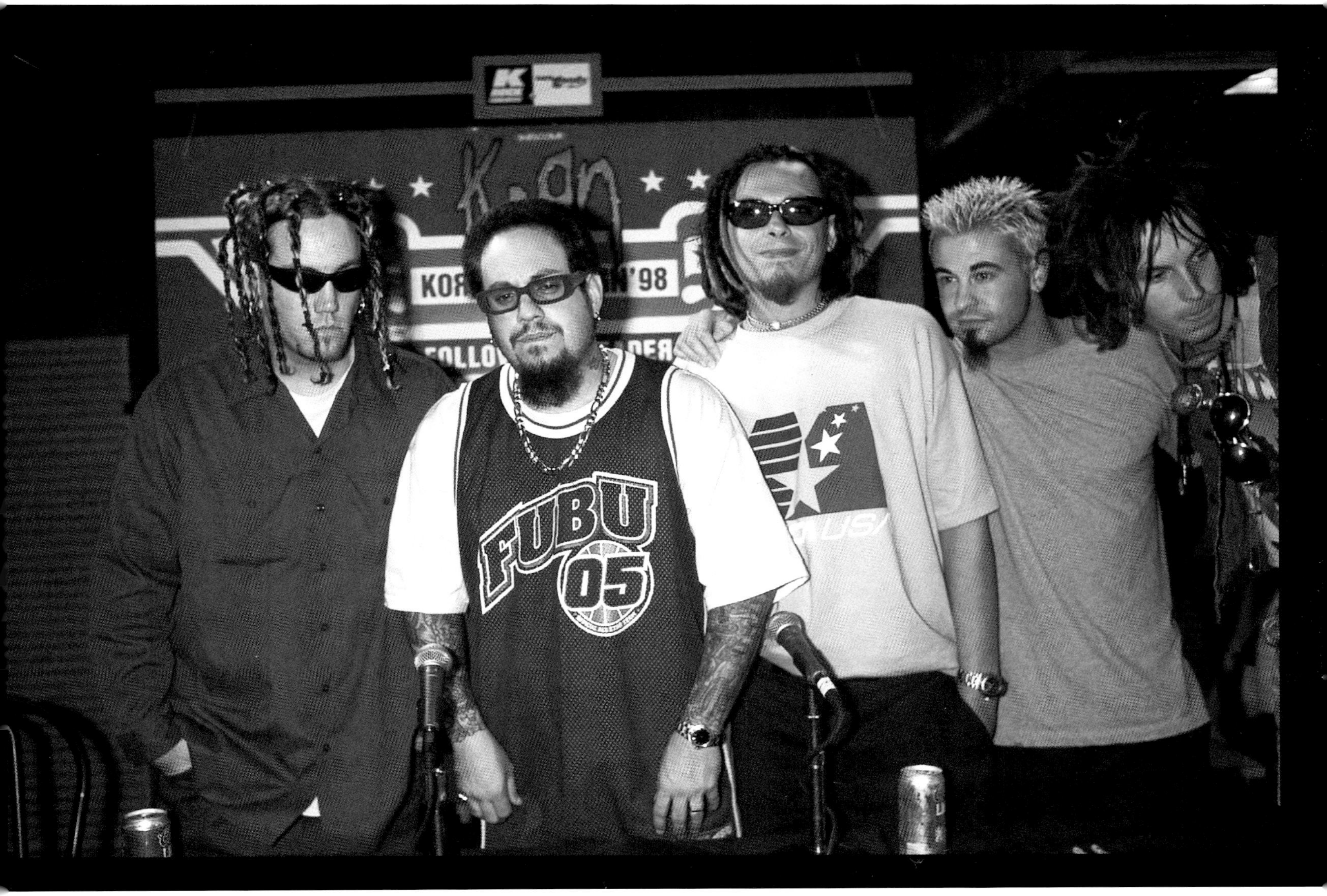
FUBU
05

ALL IN THE FAMILY

With *Follow the Leader* well on its way to multiplatinum success, Korn didn't really have anything to prove. But that's never stopped them before. The Family Values tour delivered like any close-knit, dysfunctional family of the hottest, coolest forerunners of the new sound of rock music should. It was the end-of-the-summer festival to end all summer festivals, and was destined to become as huge and as legendary as the best of them. However, before kick-starting the festivities, the members of Korn, whose mommies taught them well, just didn't feel right without paying a bit of polite homage to the true progenitor of the tour's namesake. The band sent a telegram to none other than the illustrious former Vice President Dan Quayle. "It would be entirely inappropriate and remiss of us not to extend a personal invitation to you and your family to be on-hand at any one of the tour stops on the Family Values trek. Since we believe it was you who brought the phrase 'family values' to all of our attention, this tour is somewhat of a tribute to you," the men of Korn wrote. "Listen to what you have created and look at what you have wrought. Sincerely, Korn. P.S. - 'All Excess' passes will be included with your tickets." Whether or not the Quaylemeister turned up in the mosh pit is still unconfirmed, however it was doubtless the most unusual invitation he had received in his political career. Quite an honor, really.

The onslaught of Korn, Limp Bizkit, Orgy, Ice Cube, Incubus, and pyromaniacs Rammstein slashed and burned its way across the country, opening in Rochester, New York, at the end of September and wreaking havoc on stadiums in East Rutherford (Manhattan's closest venue big enough to host the massive event), Pittsburgh, Detroit, Milwaukee, Chicago, Minneapolis, Denver, Lafayette, Kansas City, and St. Louis. The tour hit a snag in Phoenix when both Jonathan and Limp Bizkit's Fred were struck down with the flu, but the show was rescheduled and the tour barreled on through Los Angeles, San Francisco, Las Vegas, Salt Lake City, and New Orleans. A pinch of religion added a nice flavor to the Lafayette, Louisiana, gig, as one Reverend Sam Brooks and a small group of his Baptist followers reportedly prayed for protection (from that evil nasty rock music) amongst the stadium's rows of seats. Korn and company issued a statement saying, "the reverend was wasting his time, since no one sits down at a Family Values show." Indeed, some lucky fans found themselves onstage as they were imprisoned in the two-story barbed wire Korn Cage at the back of the stage. Limp Bizkit's set opened with the band emerging from a giant space ship, and Rammstein, true to their fiery reputation, employed more than a few pyrotechnics as well as a touch of simulated sodomy. Ice Cube went for the minimalist approach with an enormous statue of "Ice Cube the Great" as his sole stage ornamentation.

Korn joined forces with the Make-A-Wish Foundation yet again during the tour, meeting up with two terminally ill fans backstage. "It's kinda weird," David told *Alternative Press* in its February 1999 issue, "Out of anything they could do, they're askin' to meet us, these fuckin' guys from Bakersfield who play music." The rest of the band expressed dissatisfaction at not being able to spend enough time with eighteen-year-old Nicole and fourteen-year-old Bruce. "It's like these kids last fuckin' dream," Jonathan added. "We want to make it somethin' special for 'em."

The fabulously successful twenty-seven-date tour came to a howling Halloween night climax in Fairfax, Virginia, a stone's throw from Washington, D.C. It was a night to remember, and the time-honored concept of "trick or treat" was not forgotten. Korn threw aside the traditional store-bought superman and princess costumes and dressed up as an Eighties big-hair heavy metal outfit (complete with skin-tight spandex). They even threw a rendition of the Twisted Sister hit "We're Not Gonna Take It" into the mix. Limp Bizkit opted for a tribute to the King, in full-on Elvis Presley mode, but it was Rammstein who took the spirit of All Hallow's Eve to new heights, hitting the stage wearing nothing other than a spot of duct tape in honor, presumably, of their industrial metal genre. Unfortunately the Patriot Center officials didn't catch the reference and found the spectacle of a group of nearly nude Eastern Europeans to be wholly inappropriate for the poor innocent fans. The band was unceremoniously booted off stage. Rammstein's management later issued a statement explaining that the band

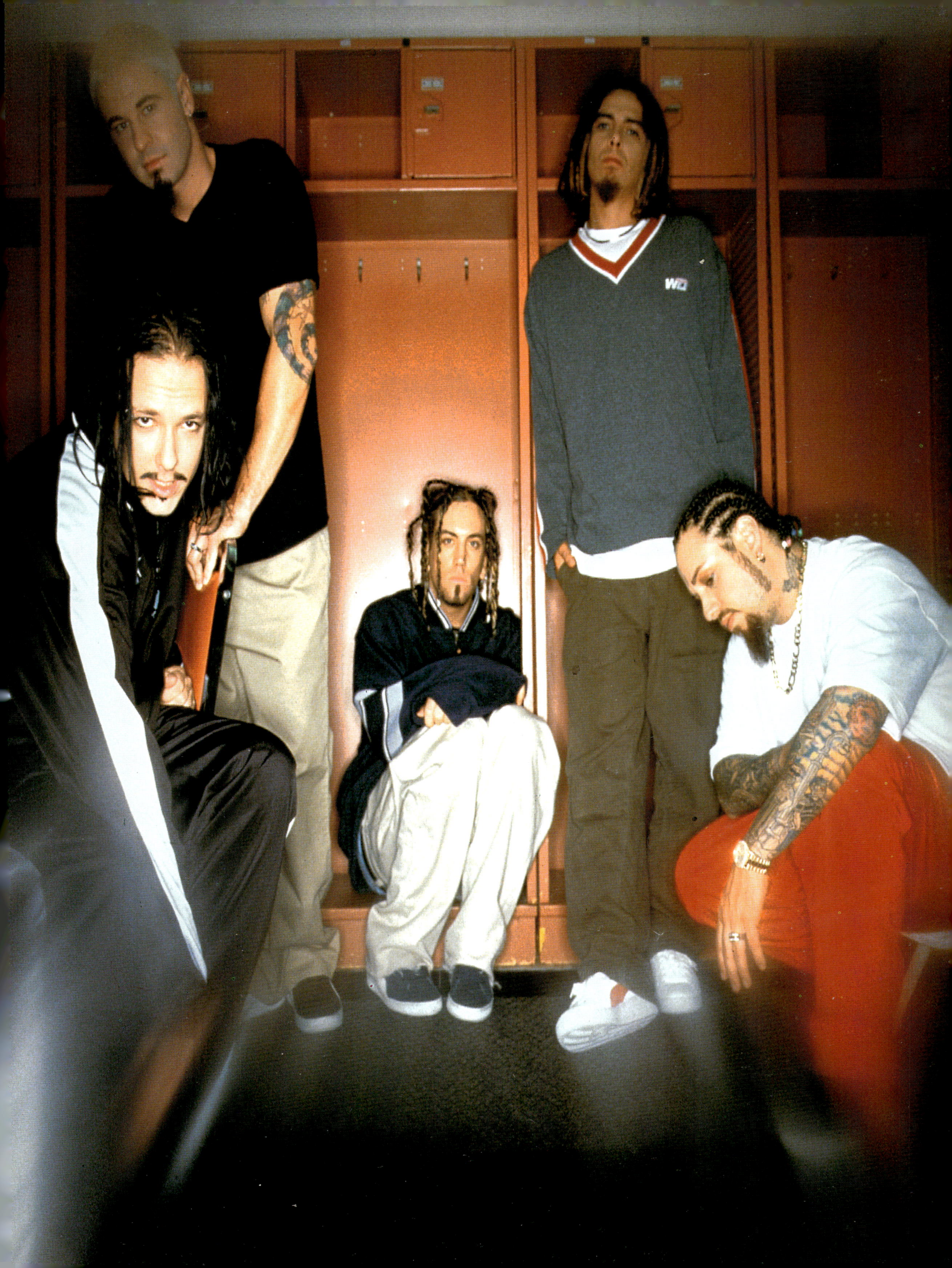

"was unaware that they were supposed to put on more clothes, instead of shedding them, on Halloween. It is a cultural difference." Even offstage, the night was not mischief-free. Korn's tour bus was involved in a dangerous Washington, D.C., highway chase in which an unidentified car attempted to run the bus off the road.

Family Values reportedly grossed more than six million dollars, but the bands—and the fans—measured its success in non-monetary terms. Munky espoused the concept of Family Values to *Guitar One* magazine in its March 1999 issue, saying, "That's one of the reasons we created the tour for ourselves: so that it was like a family. It made it much easier and less stressful." Head went on to elaborate, "We'd wake up at like three in the afternoon, see everybody, clean up, eat dinner together in catering—like a family. Then the show would start, and we'd start drinkin'." The expedition became a traveling family of sorts, and all of the bands, incredibly, got along like a house afire. Even newcomers Rammstein managed to fit in. As Orgy's Jay Gordon told *MTV News* on January 25, 1999, "We got along with them. We destroyed quite a few dressing rooms, actually, together." It was official: Family Values 1998 was the beginning of something beautiful, man.

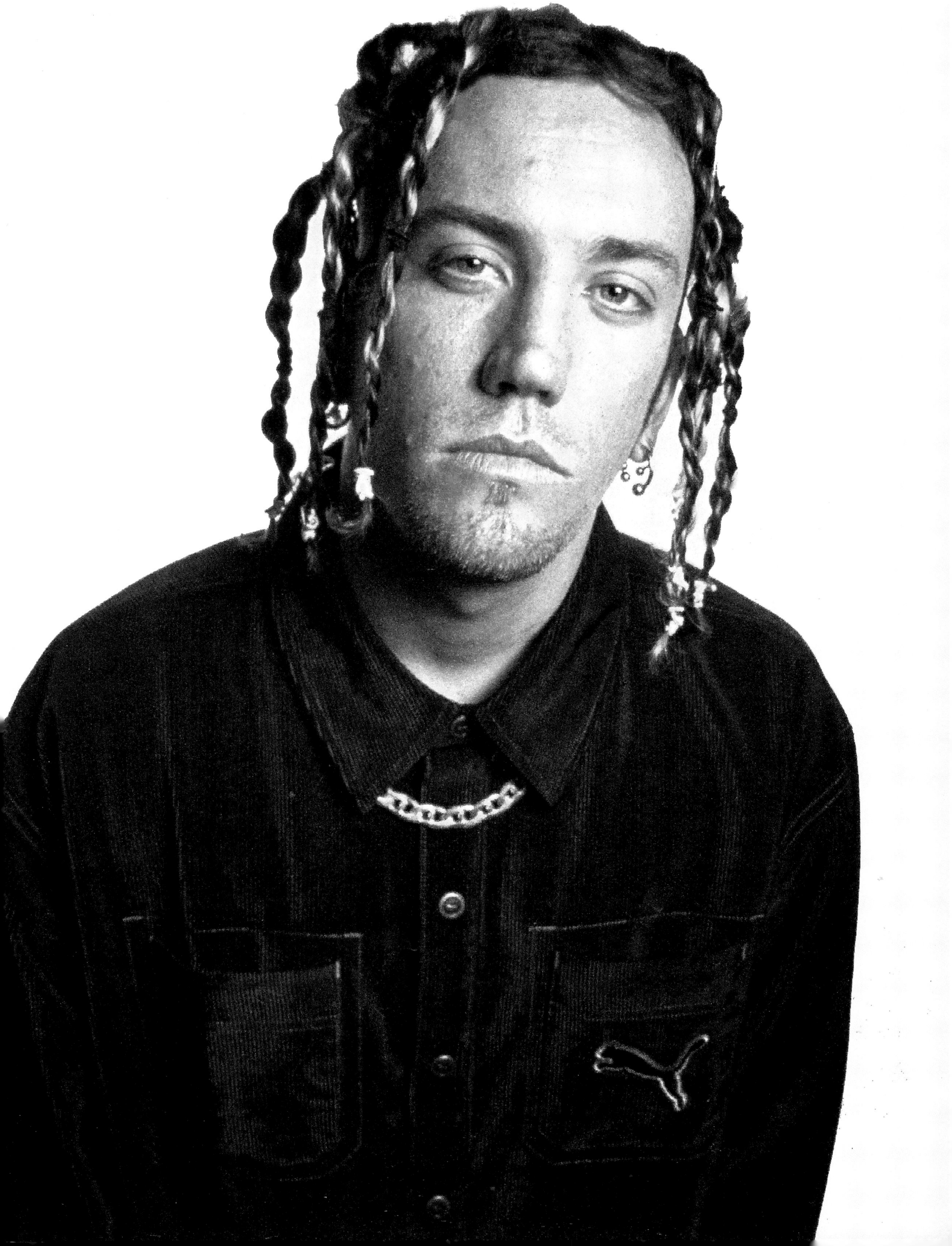

OFF THE LEASH

But there was, as there always is, trouble in paradise. The band's fabulous success, growing popularity, and critical acclaim were not stilling Jonathan's demons. His panic attacks were becoming more frequent. Jonathan's near-suicidal depression gravely effected the rest of the close-knit band. Munky later recalled sitting next to his shaking, bed-ridden friend in *Guitar* magazine's September 1999 issue, saying, "I wanted to help him so bad, but nothing I could say or do would make him come out of it. I'd tell him I love him and hold him and hug him. I'd say, 'Jon, man, all this great stuff is happening to us.' But it just didn't matter." Jonathan himself expressed concern in a summer 1998 interview published in the November Korn cover feature of *Spin* magazine, saying, "Maybe I should start taking antidepressants, or go to AA. Because when the band's joking around, the only time I feel comfortable—like I can join in—is when I'm drunk."

Jonathan was also feeling the pressures, as was the rest of the band, of being away from family. Jonathan's anger with his often-absent father during his own childhood had mellowed now that he, too, was faced with the responsibilities of fatherhood and the necessity to hit the road in order to bring home the bacon. "Ever since I've had a kid I totally have new respect for my dad. He did fuck me over, but I can understand why," he told *Spin* in its November 1998 issue. "It really freaked me out when I left to go to Japan and my son said, 'You got to go to work? Bye daddy.' Then he rolled over, like 'don't talk to me.' It hurt my feelings more than anything in the world."

It wouldn't be too long before the emotional front man finally faced his demons, giving up drinking and getting help through medication with a Prozac/Dexedrine cocktail. The first Family Values tour, unbeknownst to the fans, had turned into a hellish experience for the band. "It was fuckin' bad, dude," Jonathan revealed to *Guitar* magazine in its September 1999 issue after he had been sober for eight months. "I was going insane, literally. During Family Values, the only time I felt good was the hour that we were onstage. I was in fucking hell." Jonathan told *NME* in its November 25, 1999, issue, "I was thinking about killing myself, and I never ever thought I'd fucking say that. I would wake up every day and I couldn't get out of bed, I'd just be fucking freaking out, for no reason... My wife and I aren't together anymore, all kinds of shit. My life took a giant change then." He went on to say, "When you're really depressed it's good to hear someone be hurt too. When I get depressed I listen to my own fucking music." Cutting out the alcohol while Family Values was still in full swing also helped. "It's weird," he told *Alternative Press* in its February 1999 issue, "I've been sober for two months, and I'm havin' fun for the first time in my life." The bonus track? No more hangovers! Jonathan admits to having been apprehensive about trying medication, but proclaims that it has righted a chemical imbalance and that he is now both a sober and much happier individual, better able to deal with feelings of anger and alienation.

With barely a night off for a bit of private trick-or-treating, Korn, just two days after the Family Values Grand Finale, hit the road again. Jumping headlong into their own North American headlining show with Orgy and Incubus along for the ride, the Korn fall tour began on November 2 in Toronto, Canada. Just three dates into the tour, the Albany, New York, November 4 gig was canceled due to Jonathan being diagnosed as suffering from exhaustion. The band played on, however, and the tour carried on, finishing up in Los Angeles in December.

While in LA, Korn teamed up yet again with Todd McFarlane to work on what was to become a much-lauded breakthrough music video for the next single, "Freak on a Leash." Directed by husband-and-wife team Jonathan Dayton and Valerie Faris (whose previous video resume featured Scott Weiland and the Smashing Pumpkins), the video combined animation and live footage to brilliant effect.

Korn then decided to start the New Year off with a Down Under bang, braving the January midsummer heat at Australia and New Zealand's Big Day Out festival. The much publicized bickering between Marilyn Manson and Hole apparently spilled over to

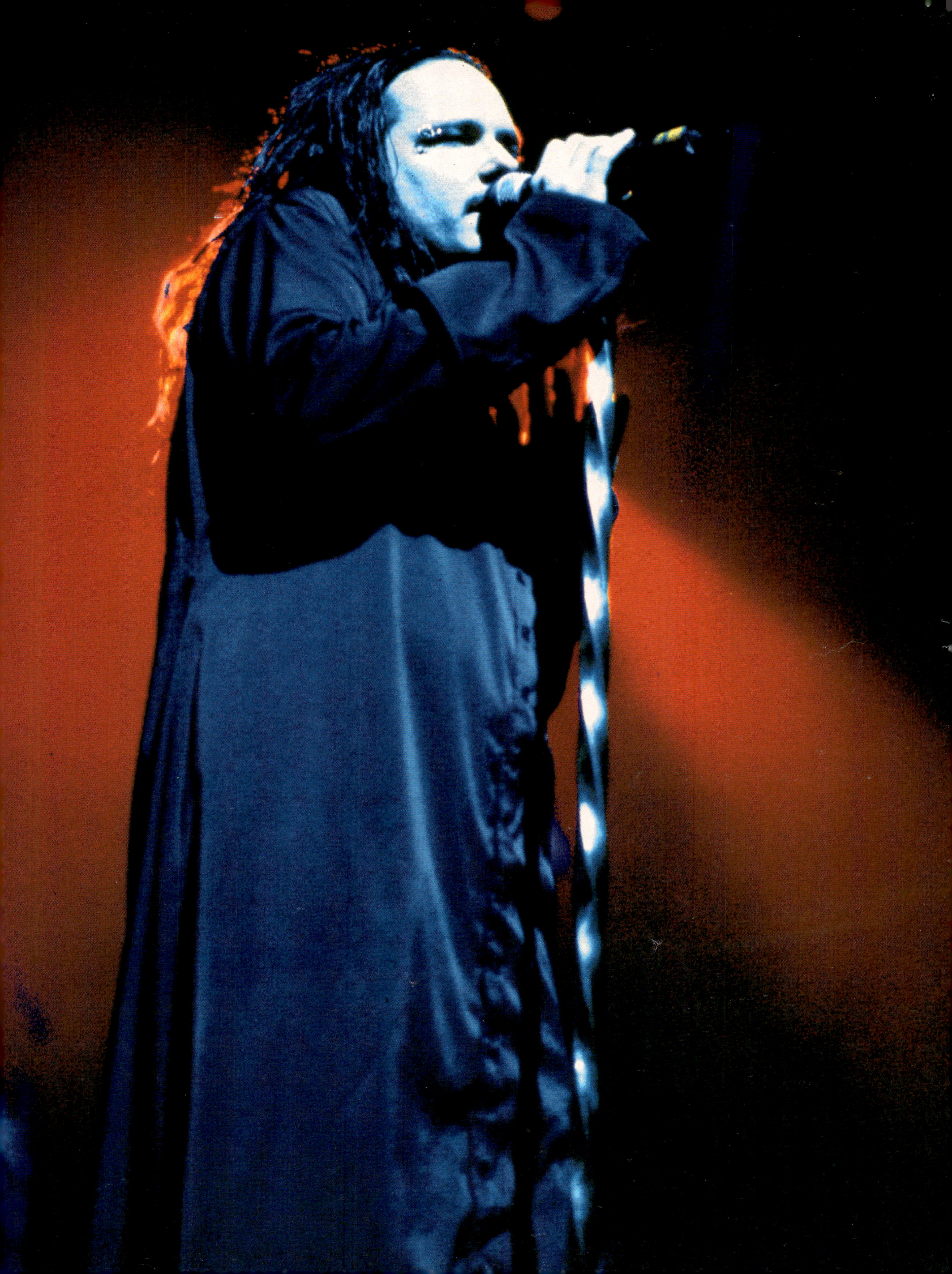

encompass innocent bystanders Korn at the Aussie event. Courtney Love put her two cents worth in to MTV News on February 12, 1999, saying, "I really like picking on Korn. I sort of turn it into an art form, and it made me really happy to pick on them, but then I realize that Jonathan is just kind of this loser, weak, sweet little guy."

"I thought it was funny because both those bands are so bitter and jealous towards us that all they did was talk about us... It was just getting ridiculous," Jonathan told *MTV News's* John Norris on March 3, 1999. Manson and Davis ended up airing their differences in public in 'you wanna step outside?' style, as Jonathan went on to recount, "Manson said a whole bunch of stuff. I actually knocked him out on stage. He called me out, he said some pretty bad things about me in front of 50,000 people and I took him out right there on stage." Now there's a show that might just be worth that twenty-four-hour plane ride to Sydney.

Korn and Rob Zombie kissed and made up to play together on the Rock Is Dead tour which commenced February 26 in Tucson, Arizona, and hit hard all across the U.S.A. before winding up in California in mid April. Korn carried on their tradition of the Korn Cage, welcomed guest stars such as Deftones' Chino Moreno, and traded instruments during their shows. Zombie's stage set was a full-on freak show in a fun house with a cast of characters including robots and grim reapers. Korn's fellow Bakersfield band Videodrone, who would sign on to Elementree Records to release their debut album (Jonathan would, in the year 2000, appear in the band's video for single "Ty Jonathan Down" along with lead singer Ty Elam), joined up as support. The only downer was Korn having to cancel two shows due to David sustaining a wrist injury, but all in all the tour was a true tour de force.

The *Family Values Tour '98* CD and video was released in March 1999. The twenty-one track live CD, featuring an intro and interludes by C-Minus as well as a "Shot Liver Medley" from Korn debuted at Number Seven, sold in excess of 121,000 copies in it first week. In its two-and-a-half star review the Los Angeles *Times* quipped, "Not quite like being there, but that's not necessarily bad." Smart asses. The CD, subtitled The *Biggest Show of Stars for '98: A Rock N' Roll Extravaganza* and recorded at both the Fairfax, Virginia, and New Orleans gigs, was a kick-ass memento of a more than memorable tour.

Meanwhile, Korn took further steps along the tightrope bridging the gap between rock and rap, working with the likes of Outkast and with Ice Cube on the single "F*** Dying." *MTV News* quoted Jonathan in a March 3, 1999, report, as saying, "It's kind of weird we're getting embraced by hip-hop now... It seems like we've opened up that gap between hip-hop and rock now. I mean it's always been there but now we're starting to throw our flavor into it." Korn would later in the year collaborate with Q-Tip (formerly of A Tribe Called Quest) on a track called "End of Times" from his solo effort *Amplified*. A bizarre side-note to the heavy/ hip-hop connection: as coincidence would have it, Q-Tip's given name was Jonathan Davis.

Korn carried on its tradition of using music to raise awareness and support important causes. A remix of "Freak on a Leash" was featured on the *No Boundaries: Benefit For The Kosovar Refugees* June 1999 benefit album featuring a diverse group of artists from Tori Amos to Neil Young. Korn signed on to the October 9 United Nations Development Program's NetAid concert, along with many big names such as Celine Dion, George Michael, Bono, Pete Townshend, Jimmy Page, Robbie Williams, Sheryl Crow, and Jewel. The concert, held at three international venues—namely New Jersey's Giants Stadium, London's Wembley Stadium, and Geneva's Palais des Nations—raised funds to aid African and Kosovar refugees.

And then it was Woodstock time. On July 23 through 25, 1999, Korn joined the ranks of Aerosmith, Bush, the Chemical Brothers, George Clinton, Collective Soul, Counting Crows, Creed, Sheryl Crow, DMX, Everlast, Fatboy Slim, Foo Fighters, Ice Cube, Jewel, Limp Bizkit, Live, the Dave Matthews Band, Metallica, Moby, Alanis Morissette, Willie Nelson, Rage Against the Machine, the Red Hot Chili Peppers, Rusted Root, the Brian Setzer Orchestra, Sugar Ray, the Tragically Hip, and more for the Thirtieth Anniversary Woodstock. Korn's blistering set was the climax of the first day of the festival, complete with fireworks and a kilt-clad Jonathan at his raging best. The *Woodstock '99* two-CD thirty-two-track set came out in October opening with a live version of "Blind" from Korn.

At the end of July, David and wife Shannon had a baby daughter named Sophia Aurora to join brother David, Jr., who reportedly had embraced the decidedly non-toddler-type pursuits of playing the drums and listening to censored versions of Korn CDs. Kids are very verbal at that age, you know, and pick up on all sorts of things—Jonathan's profanity-prone lyrics were deemed a tad inappropriate.

Lucky little David, Jr., would soon have something new to pop in his baby Walkman. July also saw the band go back into recording mode at A&M Studios in Los Angeles with producer Brendan O'Brien to work on an all-new album. O'Brien, whose previous credits (aside from working on mixing *Follow the Leader*) included Stone Temple Pilots, Rage Against the Machine, and Pearl Jam.

(seventy-one)

CULTIVATION

Follow the leader indeed—the 1999 MTV Video Music Awards at New York City's Metropolitan Opera House on September 9, 1999, further cemented Korn's reputation as forerunners of a new brand of sound. "Freak on a Leash" was nominated for a record-breaking nine awards including Video of the Year, Viewers Choice, Best Direction in a Video, Breakthrough Video, Best Art Direction in a Video, Best Special Effects in a Video, and Best Cinematography in a Video. The groundbreaking clip brought home two wins for Best Rock Video (up against Limp Bizkit, Kid Rock, Lenny Kravitz, and the Offspring) and for Best Editing in a Video (up against 2Pac, Cher, and TLC). Awards, in fact, seemed to be falling out of the sky into the collective lap of Korn. The first annual ARTISTdirect web awards showered accolades on the group in the form of the Pioneer Artist on the Internet and the Best Rock Fan Site awards. Another internet-related award came the band's way on July 19 when Korn was awarded the first CDDB Silicon CD Award. The CDDB Top Ten, an internet database that tracked which CDs were played most often on computers, declared Korn one of the hottest bands online. And to top it all off, in February 2000 Korn would finally be recognized by the Grammys. Our heroes had been overlooked in past years despite the band's success, but this year brought home a Grammy for "Freak on a Leash" for Best Music Video, Short Form.

And now, ladies and gentlemen, time again for every boy and girl's favorite festival: the Family Values Tour! Korn, having conceived of and launched the already legendary traveling showcase of the best that heavy-hitting music has to offer, opted to let their brainchild go out and play on its own this time. Handing the reins over to Limp Bizkit, Korn stayed studio-bound, dedicated to working on the follow up to *Follow the Leader*, while the second annual Family Values jump-started on September 21 in Pittsburgh, scheduled for another Halloween conclusion. With the Crystal Method, DMX, Filter, Ja Rule, Wu Tang Clan's Method Man, Mobb Deep, Primus, Redman, Run-DMC, Staind, and System of a Down on the roster, the tour promised to carry on the tried and true tradition of state of the art sold-out concerts. Jonathan explained to MTV's John Norris on August 31, 1999, that the band decided, "It would be kinda lame for us to play it every year. We wanted to just bring out new opening, new really good up and coming bands, take 'em out, and let 'em be heard."

But you know how family is: can't live with 'em, can't live without 'em, and Korn couldn't resist the temptation of hitting the stage with the Values crew; they joined up with the tour for seven dates, hitting the stage in October gigs in Grand Rapids, Indianapolis, Columbus, Rosemont, St. Louis, Kansas City, and Minneapolis. A *Family Values Tour 1999* CD featuring live versions of "Falling Away from Me" and "A.D.I.D.A.S./Good God" was soon to follow. The disturbing album artwork showcased a diaper-clad baby alternately smoking a cigarette and brandishing a rifle, accompanied by a statement from Fred Durst which read in part, "Attention: In a world where values are often forgotten we must instill them in our children. Don't be an idiot, the images you see in this book have become a reality! Kids grow into their surroundings, if you think it's ok to smoke, do drugs and drink alcohol around them think again…" summing up with a "PS Having a gun in the house with kids around is never safe."

The tour was a rousing success yet again on its second year out, and, according to *Amusement Business*, grossed over ten million dollars, a noted increase over its freshman year. No one could deny that Family Values was one hell of an idea. The Los Angeles *Times* admitted in its October 25, 1999, review of the Anaheim, California, Arrowhead Pond concert that "this combination of hard-rock, rap, and a euphoric young audience is a new tradition worth keeping."

Another tradition in the making was Korn's amazing ability to bring out album after album of innovative music, each showcasing new reaches of talent, and *Follow the Leader* was going to be a hard act to follow. However, Korn had weathered one hell of a storm during the whirlwind of their recent successes, and they found themselves gelling in the studio like never before. An amazing eight tracks came together in the first two weeks.

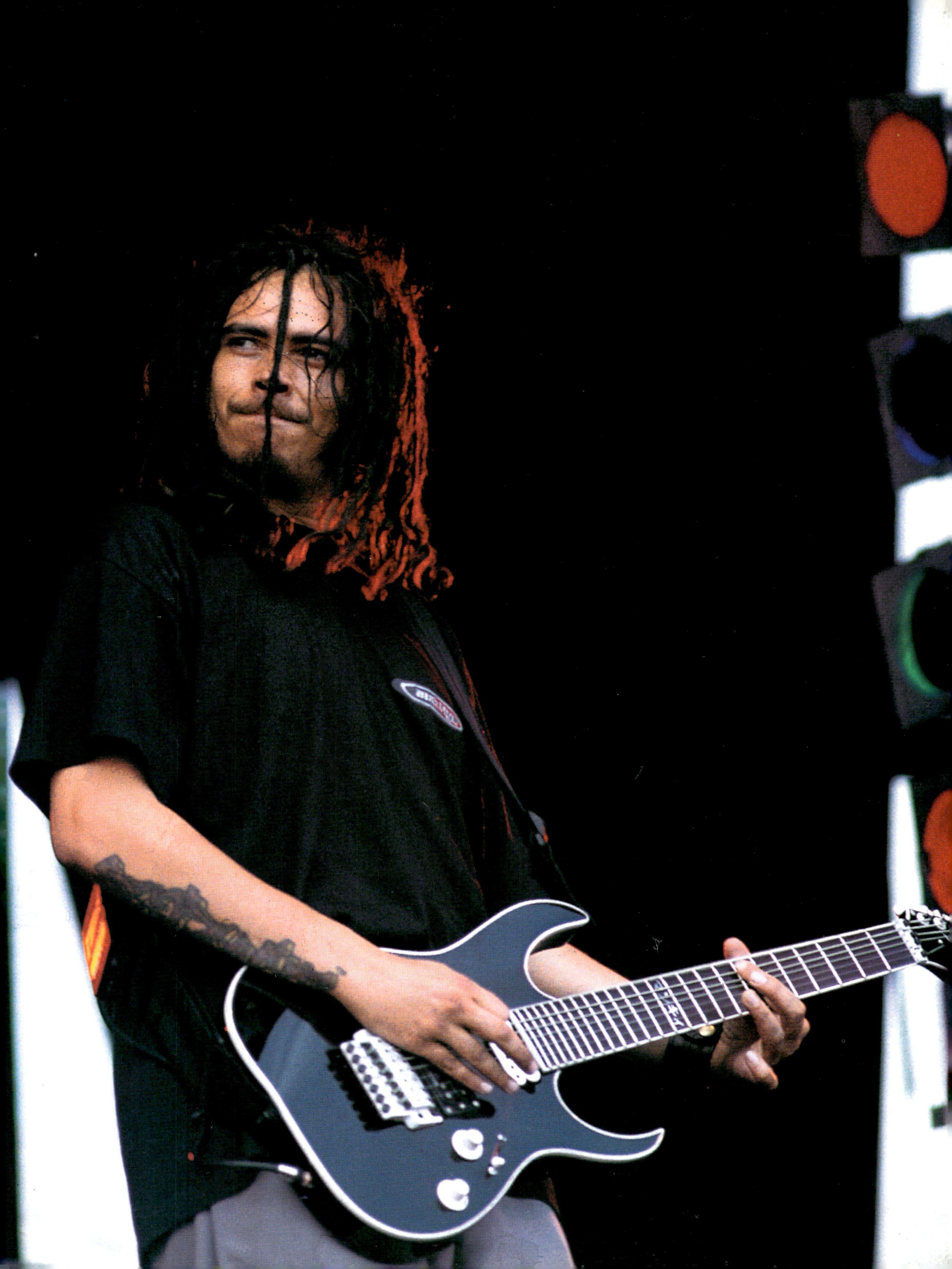

The band reportedly played around with naming the new tunes after other bands, but ultimately decided that Korn songs called "The Bangles," "Ozzy," "ZZ Top," "The Cars," and—believe it or not—"Ricky Martin" would just be too bizarre. All joking aside, the Korn foursome had a daunting task on their hands. But they weren't letting it stress them out. As Munky told *Guitar One* magazine in its March 1999 issue, "Our whole thing has always been: Just play from your heart, and then let your brain tell your hands what to do. We've always just played by whatever feels good, not by technique." And it seems that this approach may be part of the secret behind Korn's ever evolving, always experimental sound. Munky put it simply in his and Jonathan's February 2000 ARTISTdirect.com online chat, saying, "Whatever comes out of our creative thoughts, comes out into music, and then gets transferred to tape. It's a simple equation."

They may have reached never-guessed-at peaks of success, but Korn have never forgotten their ever loyal fan base, and are always thinking of new ways to involve their fans with the band's progress. Thus came the brilliant idea of asking the fans to design the band's new album cover. The MTV Korn Cover Contest had but one rule: budding artists and Korn lovers must submit square artwork to Epic Records no later than October 4, 1999. It turned out that contest winner Alfredo Carlos not only had the honor of seeing his corn-inspired rag-doll artwork grace the album's cover, he also took home a handsome $10,000 and met the band at a Northridge, California, Tower Records appearance. The band, ever fair-minded, issued limited editions of the CD featuring the artwork of each of the three contest finalists, Vince Queau, Jamil "Phoenix" Clarke, and Brad Lambert.

Korn, never ones to follow the norm, decided to launch their new single "Falling Away from Me" on—no, not MTV… no, not a major radio station… no, not at a high-profile music-industry party—the irreverent Comedy Central series *South Park*. Animated versions and the bona fide voices of Jonathan, Head, Munky, Fieldy, and David joined the cast of the show that also refuses to follow the rules in, appropriately enough, its Halloween special.

To further rock the boat of conventionality, Korn decided (against the advice of attorneys and record-industry bigwigs, of course) to give its new single away. A statement on www.korn.com read "Hey Fuckers! Let's start a fuckin' chain email!! Our new record, *Issues*, will hit the stores on November 16. We busted our asses on this record and we think this is the best shit we've ever done! We're so psyched about it that we wanted to give all you guys, the TRUE Korn fans, a gift from us." The web statement went on to offer an unprotected, no time-out MP3 file of "Falling Away from Me" and urged fans to pass it on via email to ten friends. The band set up a guest book, and for every fan who downloaded the single and signed in, the band, along with ARTISTdirect.com, vowed to donate twenty-five cents to Childhelp USA and Children of the Night, charities who are part of the battle against child abuse. The statement wrapped up with "Thanks again for everything you have done for us. Our fans are the reason we continue to make music. Korn fans rule!"

(seventy-four)

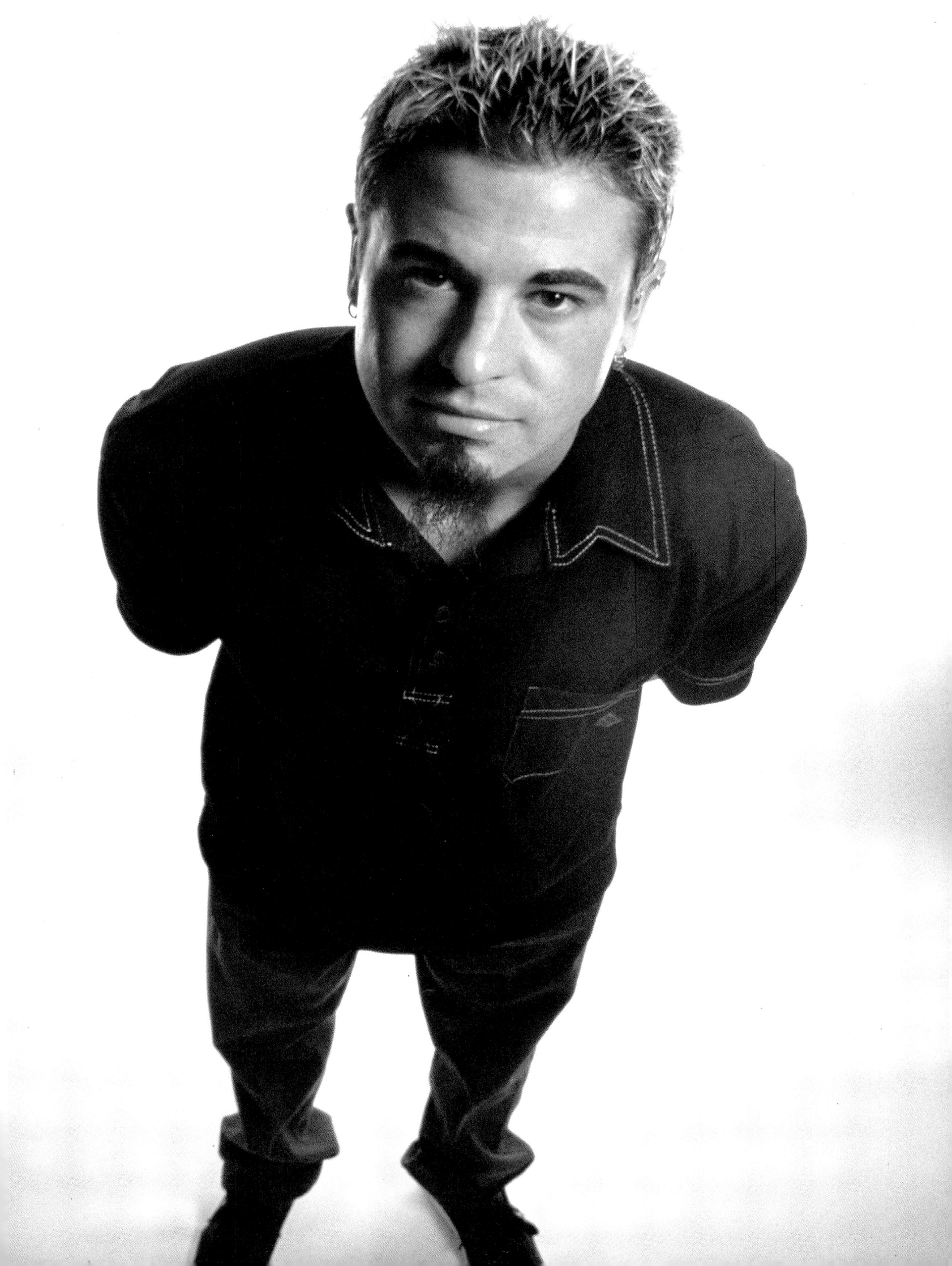

SPEAKING IN TONGUES

How to top this? How about staging a celebratory gig the night before your new album hits the stores in which you debut the entire album by performing it live? Sounded good to Korn. They chose the renowned Apollo Theatre in New York City's Harlem, which had hosted many a soul, jazz, blues, and R&B legend including Aretha Franklin, Smoky Robinson, and the one and only James Brown for the *Issues* debut concert. They asked the city's Police Department Emerald Society Pipes and Drums/New York's Fraternal Order of Police Celtic Marching Band to join them, along with a full-fledged choir. Jonathan donned his best kilt for the occasion, and the stage was moodily candelabra-lit. Of course, leave it to Korn not to be content with offering their new album, track by track, live to a select group of radio-contest-winners and ticket-buyers. They just had to broadcast the entire evening live over the web via korn.com and, for the computer-impaired, over radio stations worldwide. These guys are too fucking sweet! The November 15 show drew a few celebrities as well, and in amongst the crowd was Puff Daddy, Busta Rhymes, Chris Rock, Matt Pinfield, and ole pal Fred Durst.

Speaking of fans, we all know how loyal Korn fans are, but a couple of them apparently went a bit too far when they allegedly started what turned into a 4,300 acre fire in Ojai Valley, California, on December 21, 1999, after placing what the Los Angeles *Times* Ventura County Edition described as "a collection of bottle rockets and other illegal fireworks" inside a neighbor's mailbox who had failed to return a borrowed Korn CD. Kids, don't try this at home.

Issues was released the morning after the big party, and beat out album debuts from Dr. Dre, Celine Dion, and Will Smith to sail straight in at Number One, selling over 573,000 copies in its first week. Reviews were admiring, but still uncertain what to make of the band—which is just the way Korn likes it. The Los Angeles *Times* gave the album two and a half stars, declaring that "The real progress is in the music, the richest array of sounds the band (including Davis's shape-shifting voice) has made." Despite Korn's indisputable conquering of the U.K. market, British reviewers weren't completely won over. The venerable U.K. music magazine *Q*'s review quipped, "If Davis were to write a little self-help book it would be called *I'm Fucked, You're Fucked*," and then went on to say, "*Issues* is dark, intelligent, and very ugly. Korn may be metal's Joy Division. For so many people to like something this horrible to listen to, it must be art." The *New Music Express* review called the album "punishing, and not in a remotely pleasant way." The New York *Times* November 17, 1999, review of the Apollo gig proclaimed, "Korn has shaped one of the most popular rock archetypes of the late 1990s: the self-justifying sociopath, a character who feels so victimized and frustrated that he can't be blamed for his actions."

Opening with "Dead"—a short but far from sweet bagpipe-led sing-a-long with Jonathan chanting in a whisper *"All I want in life is to be happy"*—and closing with white noise, the album takes the listener on a sonic journey filled with melodic nuances and a fresh crop of the wholly original sounds that have thus far made Korn such a distinct voice. Punctuated by lows as frightening and piercing as its highs, *Issues* is a documentary of sorts of Korn's further spiral into its own musical universe. Jonathan's voice morphs and transfigures its way through the maze of Head and Munky's otherworldly guitars, while Fieldy and David's individual techniques expand and enhance an effect at once disparate and united. To single tracks out is difficult, as here is an album that should be heard as a whole. Suffice it to say that Korn overtook *Follow the Leader* in a single bound, leaping headlong into an entirely new plane.

Fred Durst directed and conceptualized the video for *Issue's* first single "Falling Away from Me" which deals with an issue close the band's heart: child abuse. "It was shot really well, and just stuff that kids go through, just showing it, and the whole thing of the video is to just see their salvation, basically," Jonathan explained to MTV's Kurt Loder backstage at the Apollo Theatre gig. "Our music is a release or salvation for kids to go to when they're feeling down. [The video] kind of portrays that." Dedicated Fred reportedly even postponed a Family Values gig in order to wrap the video clip and meet deadline. Of course, the two bands make a habit of trading favors; Jonathan guested on Limp Bizkit's

June 1999 sophomore effort, *Significant Other*, on the track "Nobody Like You."

The X Files-themed video for Issue's second single, "Make Me Bad," directed by Martin Weisz, featured appearances from *End of Days* and *Blade* star Udo Kier as well as überactress and Sylvester Stallone ex Brigitte Nielsen. Going to work on the video for the third single, "Somebody Someone," also directed by Martin Weisz just didn't prove to be enough for the overly energetic Korn, and they decided to put out a new video for their latest video as well. Make sense? Put it this way: the "Sickness in Salvation" remix (courtesy of Garbage's Butch Vig) of "Make Me Bad" was so damn good, it deserved its own video with its own extra-special special effects. The song was remixed for the *Return of the Rock* MTV companion CD to the Tommy Lee–hosted show, which also included tracks by Incubus, Machine Head, Coal Chamber, Staind, Slipknot, Kid Rock, System of a Down, and other heavy-rock heavyweights.

A well-deserved break finally followed the release of *Issues* while the band took a couple of months off to regroup and spend some time doing, well, whatever the hell they liked. Jonathan, however, still found himself wrapped up in music-related activities. He popped up at a gig at Hollywood's Viper Room along with Limp Bizkit and Orgy members who all turned up to check out Elijah Blue's (son of Gregg Allman and Cher) band Deadsy, which it is rumored may be a contender for the next signee to Elementree Records. Not used to being a spectator, he soon found himself in the studio again, this time in aid of the sad venture of laying down a track for *Strait Up*, the tribute album to the late lead singer of the band Snot, Lynn Strait, who died in a automobile accident in December 1998 while preparing for his band's latest album. A number of fellow artists were recording the tunes that would have made up the Snot album, including members of Coal Chamber, Limp Bizkit, RKL, Soulfly, Sugar Ray, and System of a Down.

Korn didn't surprise anyone when, instead of resting on their laurels, sitting on their asses, and enjoying their official status as one of rock's not-to-be-forgotten groundbreakers, they hit the road once again. A thirty-seven-date North American tour in support of *Issues* began February 18, 2000, in Lakeland, Florida, and was scheduled to wind up two months later in Kansas City on April 19. The Sick & Twisted Tour featured Staind as support, as well as the unorthodox addition of an animation segment in the form of "Spike & Mike's Sick & Twisted Festival of Animation" which in past years had brought attention to animators responsible for bringing us *Beavis & Butthead* and *Celebrity Deathmatch*. The Korn set list had partially been determined by, you guessed it, the fans, via a vote-in poll on korn.com. But all would not, unfortunately, run smoothly for the Korn crew. Trouble struck, not for the first time on the third night of the tour, when David injured his wrist yet again during the March 10 Fargo, North Dakota, show. The band put its next three shows on hold, and once they determined that David's injury was indeed serious, rescheduled with substitute drummer Mike Bordin, whose experience with Ozzy Osbourne and Faith No More was sure to come in handy.

Korn had hoped that David would be fully recovered and able to join them on the European leg of the tour commencing mid May in Milan, Italy, and rounding up a month later with an appearance at the Pinkpop Festival in the Netherlands, but it was not to be. "I hurt it from playing so many years," David said during his April 27, 2000, ARTISTdirect.com online chat. "Doctors think it is a nerve problem. I'm still getting opinions. And currently using acupuncture. And I'm doing everything I can to fix it." Although David was sorely missed, the European concerts were triumphant. *NME's* Andy Capper's Review of the May 22, 2000, sold-out Wembley Arena gig in London begrudgingly admitted that the "show went a long way towards justifying just how huge Korn have become. All for the fans, in spectacle alone, this was a great rock event."

Meanwhile, back in the good old U.S.A. rumors abounded of a joint tour featuring the powerhouse roster of Kid Rock, Korn, Metallica, Powerman 5000, and System of a Down played—believe it or not—exclusively on the speedways of America. Those who bet on the speedway bit lost their hard-earned cash, but the tour was made official in late April … and did include gigs at the Kentucky Speedway and St. Louis's Gateway International Speedway in addition to the conventional stadium venues. The twelve-date super-tour, dubbed the Summer Sanitorium Tour, was set to begin June 30 and wrap up in mid July, and tickets were sold on MTV.com. But before jumping aboard the tour bus again, how about a barbecue? Summer just wouldn't be summer without SoCal's annual KROQ Weenie Roast, and Korn showed up again for some burgers, dogs, and tunes along with usual suspects No Doubt, the Offspring, Stone Temple Pilots, Creed, as well as newcomer Eminem. This time Korn headlined the event, and delivered the goods with an after-midnight set complete with fireworks and helicopters. The Los Angeles *Times* June 19, 2000, report on the goings-on cited the bands as "tattooed, foulmouthed, and loud, loud, loud—and in the case of Korn's Jonathan Davis during the headlining set, sometimes speaking in tongues." Ah well, the crazy kids liked it.

So what the hell next? Korn members seem to cram several lifetimes into one, and they aren't slowing down in their old, multiplatinum age. David has branched out into modeling and acting, stepping out from behind his drum set to join fellow musicians Dave Navarro (he of Jane's Addiction and the Red Hot Chili Peppers), Poison's Bret Michaels, John Doe of X, and, er, Rick Springfield of "Jesse's Girl" and *General Hospital* fame in an acting stint on the TV cop drama *Martial Law*. David's role was as part of a gang of fugitives who kidnap Arsenio Hall. Now there's one rerun worth catching. David's good lucks and washboard abs did not escape the attention of the powers that be, and thus Korn and Klein struck up a deal. As David explained during his April 27, 2000, ARTISTdirect.com online chat, "I have a friend that works for Calvin Klein, and they asked me if I would like to do an ad. I am working on doing some movies, and doing the ads was a good way to get the attention from the movie industry. That's why I did it. And I guess my wife likes it." Tell it like it is, man. Jonathan, meanwhile, has delved a bit further into his, well, interest for all things dark when he signed on to co-write the film score along with composer Richard Gibbs for the forthcoming movie *Queen of the Damned*, based on Anne Rice's Vampire Chronicles novel of the same name. Gibbs, who conducted the choir at the *Issues* Apollo gig, is also known for his work with Robert Palmer, Chaka Khan, and the mighty Aretha Franklin, to name a few. Munky and Head are to join in, as well as Limp Bizkit's bassist Sam Rivers. Rumors of Fieldy putting out a solo hip-hop album are still flying around town. But mainly, Korn is set to continue what they started back in Bakersfield.

The band that has obviously never heard the term "summer vacation" is then slated to dive headlong into yet another tour, this time on a Korn/Powerman 5000 double bill with Papa Roach as support which won't screech to a halt until the end of August. Oh, and don't forget Family Values 2000. And don't blink, because Korn does not intend to lay low anytime soon—they are slated to get right back in the studio again in October to start brainstorming for a new album. The Korn explosion may have detonated far below ground, but the cracks are spreading across the surface at a furious pace.

THE END

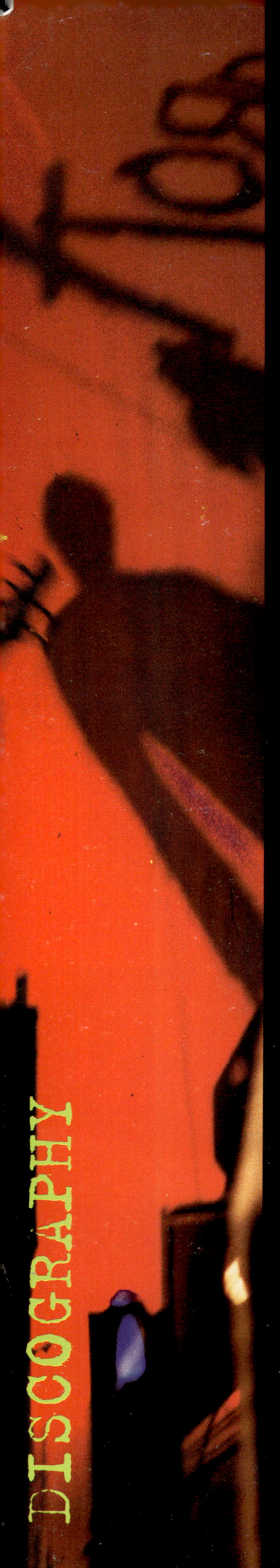

ALBUMS
L.A.P.D.
WHO'S LAUGHING NOW
Triple X Entertainment
May 3, 1991
CD: 51056-2, 02107510562 / Cassette: 51056-4,
02107510564 / LP: 51056-1, 02107510561

KORN
KORN
Epic/Immortal
October 4, 1994
CD: EK-66633, 07464666332 / Cassette: ET-66633, 07464666334
Blind/Ball Tongue/Need To/Clown/Divine/Faget/Shoots and Ladders/Predictable/Fake/Lies/Helmet in the Bush/Daddy

KORN
LIFE IS PEACHY
Epic/Immortal
October 15, 1996
CD: EK-67554, 07464675542 / Cassette: ET-67554, 07464675544
Twist/Chi/Lost/Swallow/Porno Creep/Good God/Mr. Rogers/K@#%!/No Place To Hide/Wicked/A.D.I.D.A.S./Low Rider/Ass Itch/Kill You

KORN
FOLLOW THE LEADER
Epic/Immortal Records
August 18, 1998
CD: EK-69001, 07464690012 / Cassette: 69001, 07464690014
It's On!/Freak on a Leash/Got The Life/Dead Bodies Everywhere/Children of the Korn/B.B.K./Pretty/All In the Family/Reclaim My Place/ Justin/ Seed/ Cameltosis/My Gift to You

KORN
ISSUES
Epic/Immortal
November 16, 1999
CD: EK63710 / Clean Version CD: 62239 / UK Bonus CD: 496359
Dead/Falling Away from Me/Trash/4U/Beg for Me/Make Me Bad/It's Gonna Go Away/Wake Up/Am I Going Crazy/Hey Daddy/Somebody Someone/No Way/Let's Get This Party Started/Wish You Could Be Me/Counting/Dirty

U.S. SINGLES
Blind: US Promotional Release

NEED TO: US Promotional Release
Need To

CLOWN US: Promotional Release: ESK 7735
Clown (Radio Edit)

SHOOTS AND LADDERS: US Promotional Release: ESK 7116
Shoots and Ladders (Radio Edit)/Sean Olson (Radio Edit)

A.D.I.D.A.S.: US 12": 49K 78530
A.D.I.D.A.S. (Synchro Dub)/A.D.I.D.A.S. (Under Pressure Mix)/A.D.I.D.A.S. (The Wet Dream Mix)/Wicked (Tear The Roof Off Mix)

A.D.I.D.A.S.: US Promotional Release: ESK 9133
A.D.I.D.A.S. (radio edit)

ALL IN THE FAMILY: US Promotional Release: ESK 41289 81
All In The Family (Album Version)/All In The Family (Clark World Remix)/All In The Family (Sowing The Beats Mix)/All In The Family (Beats In Peace Mix)/All In The Family (Scary Bird Mix)

GOT THE LIFE: US CD: 630229
Got the Life/Got the Life/Got the Life/I Can Remember

GOT THE LIFE REMIXES (DeeJay Punk-Roc)
US LP: 6663912

NO PLACE TO HIDE
No Place to Hide/Sean Olson/Lies

GOOD GOD
Good God/Good God/Need to (Live)/Divine(Live)

UK SINGLES
BLIND: UK 10" vinyl
Blind/Fake/Sean Olson

NO PLACE TO HIDE: UK CD1: 663845 2
No Place To Hide (Album Version)/Sean Olson/Proud (previously unreleased)

NO PLACE TO HIDE
UK CD2: 663845 5
No Place To Hide (Album Version)/Shoots and Ladders (Hip Hop Mix)/Shoots and Ladders (Industrial Mix)

NO PLACE TO HIDE
UK 7" single
No Place To Hide (Album Version)/Proud (previously unreleased)

A.D.I.D.A.S.: UK CD1: 664204 2
A.D.I.D.A.S. (radio edit)/Chi (live)/Ball Tongue (live)/Lowrider/Shoots and Ladders (live)

A.D.I.D.A.S.: UK CD2: 664204 5
A.D.I.D.A.S. (Album Version)/Faget /Porno Creep/Blind

A.D.I.D.A.S.: UK 12" vinyl
A.D.I.D.A.S. (radio edit)/Chi (live)/ Lowrider/ Shoots and Ladders (live)

GOOD GOD: UK CD1: 664658 2
Good God (Album Version)/Good God (Mekon Mix)/Good God (Du Pistols Mix)/Wicked (Tear The Roof Off Mix)

GOOD GOD: UK CD2: 664658 5
Good God (Album Version)/A.D.I.D.A.S. (Synchro Dub)/A.D.I.D.A.S. (Under Pressure Mix)/A.D.I.D.A.S. (The Wet Dream Mix)

GOOD GOD: UK 12" vinyl
Good God/Good God/A.D.I.D.A.S./A.D.I.D.A.S

GOT THE LIFE : UK CD1: 666391 2
Got The Life/Got The Life (Deejay Punk-Roc Remix)/Got The Life (D.O.S.E. Woollyback Remix)

GOT THE LIFE : UK CD2: 666391 5
Got The Life/I Can Remember/Good God (OOMPH! vs Such A Surge Rem

GOT THE LIFE : UK 12" vinyl: 666391 2
Got The Life (Deejay Punk-Roc Remix)/Got The Life (D.O.S.E. Woollyback Remix)/Got The Life

AUSTRALIAN SINGLES
GOOD GOD
Australian CD: 664387 2
Good God (Clean Version)/Need To (Live)/Good God (Album Version)/Good God (Heartfloor Mix)/Divine (Live)/Good God (Such a Surge Mix

GOT THE LIFE
Australian CD: 66343

FREAK ON A LEASH
Australian CD-ROM: 666856

FALLING AWAY FROM ME
Australian CD: 66836

EUROPEAN/INTERNATIONAL SINGLES
NO PLACE TO HIDE
No Place to Hide (Album Version)/Sean Olson (Radio Edit)/Lies

SHOOTS AND LADDERS: THE DUST BROTHERS MIXES
Hip-Hop Remix/Hyper Remix/Industrial Remix/Industrial Instrument

FALLING AWAY FROM ME (Part One & Part Two)
International CD: 668869

MAKE ME BAD
International CD: 669191

FRENCH SINGLES
GOOD GOD
EPC 664918 2
Good God (Marc Em Remix)/Good God (Oneyed Jack Remix)/Good God (Headknot Remix)/A.D.I.D.A.S. (Synchro Dub)/Good God (Album Version)

GERMAN SINGLES
A.D.I.D.A.S.
CD: 664053

NO PLACE TO HIDE
No Place to Hide/Proud/Lies

SOUNDTRACK/BENEFIT/LIVE COMPILATION ALBUMS
THE CROW: CITY OF ANGELS SOUNDTRACK
Hollywood Records 1996
CD: 2061-62047-2, 72061620472 / Enhanced CD: 2061-62074-2, 72061620742 / Cassette: 2061-62047-4, 72061620474
Sean Olson

I KNOW WHAT YOU DID LAST SUMMER SOUNDTRACK
Sony/Columbia 1997
Proud

SPAWN SOUNDTRACK
Epic 1997
CD: 68404
Kick the P.A. (Korn with the Dust Brothers)

END OF DAYS SOUNDTRACK
Geffen 1999
CD: 90508
Camel Song

NO BOUNDARIES: A BENEFIT FOR THE KOSOVAR REFUGEES
Epic 1999
CD: 6365328 Cassette: 6365342
Freak on a Leash

FAMILY VALUES: THE BIGGEST SHOW OF STARS FOR '98
Immortal/Epic 1999
CD: EK69904
Shot Liver Medley (Shoots and Ladders/Justin/Predictable/Ball Tongue/Divine/Kill You)/Freak on a Leash/Twist-Chi/Got the Life

FAMILY VALUES TOUR 1999
Flawless/Geffen 2000
CD: 069490641-2
Falling Away from Me/A.D.I.D.A.S-Good God